D0537146

Microwave Browning and Searing with
Micro-Browner® Grill
COOKBOOK

from
LITTON

contents

Introduction
3

Microwave Browning Grill Time Chart
7

Meals
8

Appetizers
16

Main Courses
24

Sandwiches and Breads
40

Eggs
48

Vegetables
54

Desserts
62

Index
69

The photographs in this book illustrate the recipes as prepared using the Micro-Browner® grill from Litton.

Pictured on cover: Grilled Family Steak, page 29; Home-Style Potato Patties, page 57; Golden Mushrooms, page 60.

⊞ LITTON

Greetings from Litton . . .

Just like the frosting on a special cake, the golden brown finishing touch that makes good-tasting microwaved foods taste and look even better is available with Litton's new family-sized Micro-Browner® Grill.

As you read and cook your way through this easy-to-follow cookbook and grilling guide, you will be impressed with the flexibility and uniqueness of this brand new family sized Micro-Browner Grill for browning, searing, roasting and/or grilling, for all types of food, from cocktail tidbits to tenderloins.

Golden bread loaves, toasty sandwiches, sautéed vegetables, grilled meats and even desserts – there are detailed, simple to follow instructions and mouth-watering menu ideas in all catagories of good eating.

All recipes have been carefully tested in our Litton Microwave Ovens with a power output of 600 to 650 watts, and are designed for use with this Micro-Browner only.

We at Litton strive daily to make microwave cooking easier and more enjoyable for you. All of our products, from ovens to cookbooks, are designed to fulfill your cooking needs. Because your opinions count with us, we would like to hear from you if you have any ideas or questions. Just write:
Litton Microwave Cooking, 1405 Xenium Lane, Minneapolis, Minnesota 55441.

LITTON MICROWAVE COOKING CENTER

about the microwave browning grill

Your microwave browning grill functions much like a conventional frying pan or grill. The surface of the grill is preheated. Then, as foods are added they sizzle and brown just as they do in a heated skillet.

Foods cooked in a microwave oven are tender, juicy and flavorful, because they are cooked quickly and without heating the inside of the oven. Large food items, such as roasts, turkey and chicken do brown in the microwave oven through the cooking of their natural fats and juices. But because there is no heat in the microwave oven, some applications of smaller food items — browning, searing and grilling steaks and hamburgers, for example, or frying eggs, do not naturally brown in a microwave oven. The microwave browning grill provides the capability for browning, searing, grilling and frying — during microwave cooking. Your microwave oven and kitchen remain cool, yet you enjoy the appetizing appeal of conventionally broiled foods — prepared with the speed of your microwave oven and at a fraction of the cost of operating your conventional broiler or grill!

how does the microwave browning grill brown?

The grill is made of a specially formulated ceramic material with a unique coating on the underside. Unlike most glass dishes, which allow microwaves to readily pass through them with no effect, the special coating on the grill absorbs microwave energy. By placing the empty grill in the oven for preheating, the microwaves are absorbed by the surface and the grill becomes very hot. When foods are placed on the grill, the hot surface begins the browning process. When the grill is returned to the oven to cook the food, the food absorbs most of the microwaves and browning continues.

what happens during browning?

The food on the first side quickly browns from the heat stored in the grill surface during preheating. Microwaves are used during browning to quickly heat and cook the parts of the food not in direct contact with the hot surface. As juices cook from the food, some are evaporated from the hot surface and others drain into the well. The food is usually brownest on the first side since the grill is hottest when browning that side.

are preheat times the same for all foods?

No, preheat times vary depending upon the types of food. The more browning desired (as for meats), the longer preheat time is necessary. Also, the more food on the grill and the colder the food is before browning, the more preheat time is necessary.

will foods stick to the grill surface?

Some foods with little natural fat on the surface will stick. Simply lightly butter the food, use a non-stick vegetable coating or grease lightly to prevent sticking. Butter, we find, enhances both the browning and flavor of lean meats, breads, cakes and vegetables.

how do I clean the microwave browning grill?

Soap and hot water is adequate for most cleaning. The grill can be immersed in water and placed in automatic dishwashers just as any glass ceramic casserole. For more stubborn stains, a *plastic* scouring pad and baking soda or household cleanser can be used on the top side. However, do not use the cleanser on the underside since it may harm the coating.

special hints to remember in using the grill

Use times in recipes or time chart for preheating and reheating grill.

●

Be sure the food is completely thawed before searing it on the grill. Ice crystals remaining in the food will prevent browning.

●

Foods on the grill are always cooked uncovered.

●

Either plastic or metal spatulas can be used.

●

Fats and juices may spatter when cooking meats, but they are easily wiped off the oven after cooking.

●

Well will hold drippings from most foods. If foods are especially fatty or juicy and several batches are being cooked, it may be necessary to empty well between batches.

●

Scrape drippings from grill surface into well before reheating grill.

●

Hot grill can be placed directly on most kitchen counter tops, but use care in placing on table tops. Heat is trapped on the underside of dish and can cause damage.

●

The grill surface becomes very hot when preheated. Never touch the hot surface or underside of the grill when in use.

●

If food doneness is just right after cooking, be sure to remove food from grill to avoid overcooking.

●

Don't use a sharp knife for cutting on the grill since it may scratch the surface. However, surface scratches will not affect performance.

●

Handles are usually cool enough to touch, but with longer cooking times or when well contains drippings it may be necessary to use hot pads for safe handling.

●

Grill can be immersed in water while still hot, but it will be easier to handle if cooled slightly before immersing.

●

Avoid using grill in conventional oven or placing directly over burner of conventional range.

●

Expect to see some smoking with the microwave browning grill as in conventional broiling.

●

As with any ceramic cooking utensil, the microwave browning grill may break when dropped or struck sharply against a solid surface.

easy steps
to microwave grill
browning

I

To preheat, place the empty microwave browning grill in the microwave oven. Microwave on 'HIGH' (or COOK), set the timer and operate oven just like when you're cooking.

2

If butter or oil is required, apply it to the microwave browning grill.

3

Place the food on the preheated grill, set the timer, and cook for time specified for first side.

4

Turn the food over to brown the other side. (Most, but not all foods, are browned on two sides.) Set the timer and cook the second side as directed.

5

Before browning additional foods, scrape any excess drippings and food particles from grill surface into the well and reheat the grill for time specified (usually ½ to ⅔ the original preheat time). Once the grill is reheated, continue as for the original batch.

USER INSTRUCTIONS
PRECAUTIONS TO AVOID POSSIBLE EXPOSURE
TO EXCESSIVE MICROWAVE ENERGY

(a) Do not attempt to operate this oven with the door open since open-door operation can result in harmful exposure to microwave energy. It is important not to defeat or tamper with the safety interlocks.

(b) Do not place any object between the oven front face and the door or allow soil or cleaner residue to accumulate on sealing surfaces.

(c) Do not operate the oven if it is damaged. It is particularly important that the oven door close properly and that there is no damage to the: (1) Door (bent), (2) hinges and latches (broken or loosened), (3) door seals and sealing surfaces.

(d) The oven should not be adjusted or repaired by anyone except properly qualified service personnel.

microwave browning grill time chart

Food Item	Amount	Preheat Time	Special Techniques	Microwave First Side	Microwave Second Side
Appetizers					
Canapés	16	4 min.	Butter bread	1-1½ min.	—
Meatballs	25 (1 lb.)	5 min.	1-inch balls	1½ min.	1-1½ min.
Pizza Rolls	6-oz. pkg.	5 min.	Frozen	1 min.	1½-2 min.
Meats					
Bratwurst	1 lb.	8 min.	—	3 min.	4-5 min.
Canadian Bacon	6 slices	8 min.	Cut ¼-inch thick	1½ min.	1½-2 min.
Family Steak	2 lb.	9 min.	Use tenderizer	6 min.	5-7 min.
Filets Mignons	4 (6-oz. each)	9 min.	Butter grill	5 min.	4-5 min.
Flank Steak	1½-lb.	8 min.	Marinate	3 min.	3-4 min.
Ham Slices	1½ lbs.	7 min.	Cut ½-inch thick	1½ min.	1-2 min.
Hamburger Patties	1-1½ lbs.	8 min.	Form 4 to 6 patties	4 min.	3-6 min.
Lamb Chops	6 rib chops	8 min.	Cut 1-inch thick	8 min.	7-8 min.
Lamb Patties	1½ lbs.	8 min.	Form 6 patties	2½ min.	2-3 min.
Meatballs	12 (1 lb.)	8 min.	1½-inch balls	2 min.	3½-4½ min.
Minute Steaks	1 lb.	8 min.	Butter grill	4 min.	4-5 min.
Pork Chops	4 chops	8 min.	Cut ½-inch thick	9 min.	10-12 min.
Smoked Pork Chops	4 chops	8 min.	Cut ½-inch thick	6 min.	6-7 min.
Sausage Links	11 links	8 min.	—	1 min.	2-3 min.
Sausage Patties	12 ozs.	8 min.	10 slices	1½ min.	2½-3½ min.
Sirloin Steak	2 lb.	9 min.	Butter grill	5 min.	1-2 min.
T-Bone Steaks	2 (8-oz. each)	9 min.	Butter grill	5 min.	1-2 min.
Veal Cutlets	1½ lbs.	8 min.	Bread chops	2 min.	2½-3½ min.
Wieners	10	8 min.	—	1 min.	1-1½ min.
Chicken, Fried	2½-lb.	8 min.	Quartered	10 min.	15-17 min.
Fish Fillets, Fresh	1½ lbs.	8 min.	Butter Grill	2 min.	1½-2 min.
Fish Sticks, Frozen	8-oz. pkg.	7 min.	Butter grill	2 min.	1½-2 min.
Fish Portions, Frozen	1-lb. pkg.	7 min.	Butter grill	3 min.	2-3 min.
Salmon Steaks	4 steaks	8 min.	Butter grill	2½ min.	3-3½ min.
Eggs, Fried	1-2 eggs	5 min.	Butter grill	¾-1½ min.	—
	3-5 eggs	5 min.	Use foil rings	2-4 min.	—
Sandwiches					
Grilled	4	5 min.	Butter bread	1 min.	1-1½ min.
Open-Faced	4	5 min.	Butter bread	1½-2 min.	—
Pizza, Frozen	10-inch	5 min.	—	5-6 min.	—
Breads					
Biscuits, refrig.	10	5 min.	Dip in butter	¾ min.	¾-1 min.
French Toast	4-6 slices	5 min.	Butter grill	½ min.	1-1½ min.
Garlic Toast	8 slices	5 min.	Brush with butter	1½ min.	1½-2 min.
Pancakes	2-3	5 min.	Butter grill	¾ min.	1-1½ min.
Vegetables					
Cabbage Wedges	6 wedges	5 min.	Brush with butter	2 min.	2½-3 min.
Mushrooms, Fresh	8 ozs.	5 min.	Butter grill	1 min.	1-2 min.
Potatoes, sliced	4 med.	5 min.	Butter grill	5 min.	5-6 min.
Potato Patties	4 patties	5 min.	Butter grill	4 min.	2-3 min.
Frozen Potato Logs	16-oz. pkg.	5 min.	Butter grill	3 min.	3-4 min.
Frozen Hash Browns	12-oz. pkg.	5 min.	Precook 5-6 min.	4 min.	3-4 min.
Tomatoes, Grilled	9 slices	5 min.	Coat with crumbs	1 min.	1-1½ min.
Desserts					
Cake, Toasted	8 slices	4 min.	Spread with butter	1 min.	½-1 min.
Grilled bananas	3 bananas	5 min.	Split lengthwise	1-1¼ min.	—
Grilled pineapple	1 fresh	5 min.	Butter slices	4 min.	1-1½ min.

meal*s*

Cooking for just one or two? It takes careful shopping and practice, doesn't it, to avoid a backlog of leftovers, unnecessary dishes to wash up and the temptation to have just a snack rather than fix a nutritious meal?

But just think — with your microwave browning grill, several foods can be grilled simultaneously for breakfast, lunch or dinner! Presto — cooking for one or a few is tastefully and easily accomplished in minutes with only the browning tray to clean afterwards.

Preheat times, determined by the foods requiring the longest cooking times, are important to insure enough heat in the grill to brown all foods adequately. And, foods which overcook easily and/or need little cooking are simply added after other items are partially done and when the grill has cooled a bit. Some accompaniment foods, which take longer to cook than the meat, are precooked before grilling. Since many of these steps differ little from conventional cooking, they become second nature in no time.

The placement and rearranging of foods on the grill is also significant. So, in order that everything fits on the grill surface with ease and cooks properly as well, we have included illustrations throughout the chapter for easy-to-follow guides.

Pictured: Hamburger and Fries Lunch, page 13.

The toast "frame" keeps the egg in place on the grill.

BACON, EGG AND TOAST BREAKFAST

> **1 slice bread**
> **½ tablespoon butter or margarine, if desired**
> **2 to 3 slices bacon**
> **1 egg**

1. Preheat microwave browning grill for 5 minutes on HIGH.

2. Spread one side of bread slice with butter. Cut a 3-inch circle from center of slice, using a drinking glass or biscuit cutter.

3. Place bacon in single layer in center of preheated grill.

4. Microwave for 2 minutes on HIGH. Turn bacon over and move to one end of grill. Add bread pieces, buttered-side-down.

5. Microwave for 1 minute on HIGH. Turn bread pieces over. Break egg into hole in center of bread slice.

6. Microwave for 2 to 2½ minutes, on HIGH, or until egg is desired doneness.

1 Serving

TIPS For additional servings, reheat microwave browning grill for 3½ minutes on HIGH.

● Two eggs and toast slices can be cooked by placing partially cooked bacon atop egg and toast squares. Increase time for cooking eggs by about 1 minute.

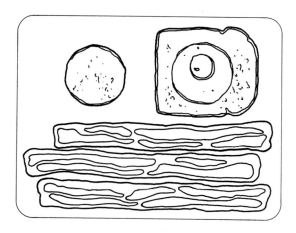

Suggested way to arrange food items on the microwave browning grill.

Either sausages are removed with first batch of pancakes or reheat time must be increased.

PANCAKE AND SAUSAGE BREAKFAST

Pancake batter for about 6 pancakes
4 sausage links
½ medium banana, sliced

1. Preheat microwave browning grill for 8 minutes on HIGH.

2. Prepare pancake batter.

3. Place sausage links in center of grill.

4. Microwave for 1 minute on HIGH. Turn links over and move to long sides of grill. Spoon 2 pancakes onto grill using a scant ¼ cup batter for each. Top with 4 or 5 banana slices, pressing into batter.

5. Microwave for 30 to 45 seconds, on HIGH, or until underside is browned. Turn pancakes over and continue cooking for 1 to 1½ minutes, on HIGH, or until done. Remove pancakes and sausage links.

6. Reheat microwave browning grill for 2 minutes on HIGH. Spoon batter for 2 or 3 more pancakes onto grill. Top with banana slices as directed in Step 4.

7. Microwave for 45 seconds on HIGH. Turn pancakes over and continue cooking for 1 to 1½ minutes, on HIGH, or until done. Repeat steps 6 and 7 for remaining pancake batter. About 2 Servings

TIPS Pancake syrup can be heated and butter softened in microwave before preheating grill.

● If pancakes have cooled before serving, just microwave for 45 to 60 seconds, on HIGH, or until heated.

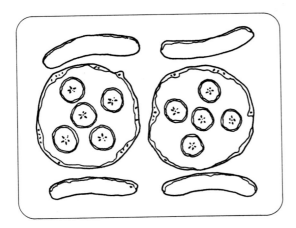

Suggested way to arrange food items on the microwave browning grill.

Grill toasts the bread, cooks the bacon, melts the cheese and even sautées the apple.

SANDWICH AND APPLE LUNCH

    1 apple, halved and cored
    1 tablespoon sugar
  ¼ teaspoon cinnamon
    3 slices bacon
    1 slice bread
    1 tablespoon mayonnaise or salad dressing
    3 tomato slices
    1 slice cheese

1. Preheat microwave browning grill for 5 minutes on HIGH.

2. Coat cut surface of cored apple with mixture of sugar and cinnamon; reserve any remaining sugar.

3. Place bacon slices in single layer on center of preheated grill.

4. Microwave for 2 minutes on HIGH. Turn bacon over and move to side of grill. Place apple halves cut-side-down on grill along with bread slice.

5. Microwave for 1½ to 2 minutes, on HIGH, or until bread is toasted. Turn bread over; spread with mayonnaise. Top with tomato slices, cheese and crumbled bacon.

6. Microwave for 1½ to 2 minutes, on HIGH, or until cheese is melted. Sprinkle apple with any remaining cinnamon-sugar mixture.   1 Serving

TIPS Use this same idea for other open-faced sandwiches made with cheese or cooked meats.

● A fresh peach or pear can be substituted for apple. Just peel before heating.

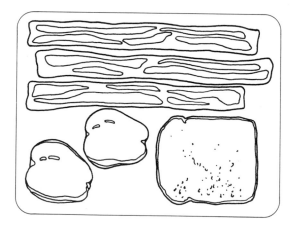

Suggested way to arrange food items on the microwave browning grill.

French fries need to be in contact with grill's hot surface to heat and become crisp by the time hamburger is cooked.

HAMBURGER AND FRIES LUNCH

> ¼ **lb. ground beef**
> **Salt and pepper**
> **1 onion slice, cut ¼-inch thick**
> **1 cup frozen French Fries**
> **1 hamburger bun, split and buttered**

1. Preheat microwave browning grill for 8 minutes on HIGH.

2. Season ground beef with salt and pepper. Shape into patty, about ½-inch thick.

3. Place meat patty and onion slice at one end of preheated grill. Place potatoes in single layer on remaining grill surface.

4. Microwave for 3 minutes on HIGH. Turn over patty, onion slice and potatoes. Move potatoes to one side so bun can be placed cut-side-down on grill.

5. Microwave for 1½ to 2 minutes, on HIGH, or until desired doneness.

1 Serving

TIP For additional servings, reheat microwave browning grill for 5 minutes.

Suggested way to arrange food items on the microwave browning grill.

Potatoes require thawing and precooking for best browning.

STEAK AND HASH BROWNS DINNER

6 oz. frozen hash brown patty
1 tablespoon butter or margarine
10 oz. steak, cut ½-inch thick
1 tomato, cut in half crosswise
Salt and pepper

1. Place hash browns in shallow glass dish or casserole. Cover with glass lid or wax paper.

2. Microwave for 3 minutes on HIGH.

3. Preheat microwave browning grill for 9 minutes on HIGH.

4. Coat surface of preheated grill with butter. Place steak and hash browns on opposite ends of grill.

5. Microwave for 5 minutes on HIGH. Turn steak and hash browns over. Place tomato on grill cut-side-down. Continue cooking for 1 to 2 minutes, on HIGH, or until steak is desired doneness. Season steak, potatoes and tomato with salt and pepper.
                                                                1 to 2 Servings

TIPS For added flavor, add 1 tablespoon chopped onion to hash browns before cooking.

• For PORK CHOP AND HASH BROWNS DINNER, substitute 2 pork chops (about 5 ozs. each) for steak. Microwave first side for 6½ minutes on HIGH. Turn chops and hash browns over and microwave for 4 minutes on HIGH. Add tomato and microwave for 1 to 2 minutes, on HIGH, or until chops are tender.

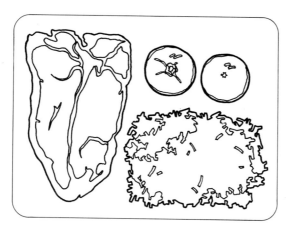

Suggested way to arrange food items on the microwave browning grill.

If you're calorie conscious, you'll be glad to know this meal contains only 350 calories.

CHICKEN BREAST WITH RICE DINNER

 ⅓ **cup water**
 ⅓ **cup quick-cooking rice**
  1 **teaspoon butter or margarine**
 ¼ **teaspoon salt**
 ½ **whole chicken breast**
  Paprika
  1 **medium zucchini, cut in half lengthwise**
  Salt and pepper

1. Microwave water in 2-cup glass measure for 1 to 1½ minutes, on HIGH, or until water boils. Add rice, butter and salt. Stir and set aside.

2. Preheat microwave browning grill for 8 minutes on HIGH. Sprinkle chicken breast with paprika.

3. Place chicken breast skin-side-down on preheated grill.

4. Microwave for 4 minutes on HIGH. Turn chicken over. Place zucchini cut-side-down on grill.

5. Microwave for 3 minutes on HIGH. Add rice and continue cooking for 3 to 4 minutes on HIGH, or until chicken is done. Season chicken and zucchini with salt and pepper.   1 Serving

TIP Leftover rice can be used. Allow about ½ cup per serving.

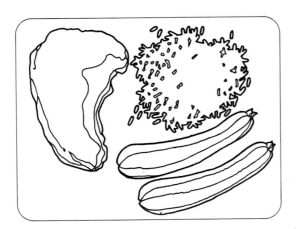

Suggested way to arrange food items on the microwave browning grill.

appetizer*r*

Appetizers — the ice breaker that can't be beat! Not only do they stimulate conversation, they whet the appetite for heartier courses to come. And, best of all, they are a delicious expression of your hospitality.

Before your guests can say, "I'll have another, thank you," the hot surface of the microwave browning grill quickly browns meat and bread tidbits while microwaves thoroughly heat them through.

Toast-based canapés are especially streamlined with the browning grill — your "secret weapon" in the kitchen. No longer is it necessary to toast bread separately before topping with your favorite spread — the grill takes care of the toasting detail while microwaves heat the topping.

Four minutes of preheating time is all that is necessary for most bread-type appetizers. And, for the meat variety, a 5-minute warm-up period is all it takes.

Ready-made frozen hors d'oeuvres, which look and taste best with a lightly browned crust, come off the grill crisp and golden to satisfy the most discerning nibbler.

Since many of the recipes can be assembled ahead (so you can enjoy your own party along with everyone else), they need only be placed on the preheated grill as company begins arriving.

For your convenience, we have included reheat times for cooking a second batch of some of the larger quantity recipes. Or, if "extras" aren't needed, just pop them in the refrigerator or freezer for a head start on your next party.

Pictured: Appetizer Meatballs, page 18; Tomato Topper Canapés, page 21; Parmesan Nibblers, page 20.

APPETIZER MEATBALLS

  1 lb. ground beef
  1 egg
  ½ cup grated Parmesan cheese
  1 teaspoon dried parsley flakes
  ⅛ teaspoon pepper
  1 teaspoon salt
  ¼ cup dry bread crumbs

1. Prepare Meatball Sauce (see below).

2. Combine all meatball ingredients in mixing bowl; mix well.

3. Preheat microwave browning grill for 5 minutes on HIGH.

4. Shape meat into 1-inch meatballs. Arrange on preheated grill.

5. Microwave for 1½ minutes on HIGH. Turn meatballs over and continue cooking for 1 to 1½ minutes, on HIGH, or until meatballs are done. Serve hot on cocktail picks with Meatball Sauce for dipping.   About 25 Meatballs

MEATBALL SAUCE

1. Combine ½ cup catsup, ¼ cup grape jelly and 2 tablespoons water in 2-cup glass measure.

2. Microwave for 1½ minutes on HIGH. Stir and continue cooking for 1 to 1½ minutes, on HIGH, or until sauce boils and jelly is melted. Serve with meatballs.   ¾ Cup

SWEET 'N SOUR KABOBS

  ½ tablespoon cornstarch
  ¼ cup packed brown sugar
  1 tablespoon soy sauce
  2 tablespoons vinegar
  5 precooked smokie link sausages
  1 can (15¼ oz.) pineapple chunks, drained

1. Combine cornstarch and brown sugar in 1-cup glass measure. Stir in soy sauce and vinegar.

2. Microwave for 1 minute on HIGH. Stir and continue cooking for 1 to 1½ minutes, on HIGH, or until mixture boils and thickens. Set aside.

3. Preheat microwave browning grill for 5 minutes on HIGH.

4. Cut each sausage into 4 pieces. Arrange pieces of sausage and pineapple chunks on toothpicks. Place on preheated grill.

5. Microwave for 1 minute on HIGH. Turn kabobs over and continue cooking for 1 to 1½ minutes, on HIGH, or until lightly browned. Serve with warm sauce.   About 20 Kabobs

Miniature cheese and ham sandwiches are a popular addition for any hors d'oeuvre tray.

CROQUE MONSIEUR

> ¼ **cup mayonnaise or salad dressing**
> 1 **tablespoon prepared mustard**
> 8 **slices bread**
> 4 **slices cooked sandwich ham**
> 4 **slices Swiss cheese**
> ¼ **cup butter or margarine, softened**

1. Combine mayonnaise and mustard; spread one side of each bread slice with mixture. Top 4 bread slices with ham and cheese slices; cover with remaining bread slices.

2. Preheat microwave browning grill for 5 minutes on HIGH.

3. Spread outside of sandwiches with butter. Arrange sandwiches on pre-heated grill.

4. Microwave for 45 seconds on HIGH. Turn sandwiches over and continue cooking for 1 to 1½ minutes, on HIGH, or until cheese is melted. Allow to stand on grill a few minutes. Remove from grill and cool slightly.

5. Place sandwiches on cutting board. Trim crusts from sandwiches and cut each sandwich into quarters. For ease in serving, secure layers of sandwich with toothpick.   16 Appetizers

TIP Ham and cheese slices should be cut just smaller than bread slices.

Quick Mexican-flavored snacks.

CHEESY TORTILLA TURNOVERS

> 1 **cup shredded Monterey Jack cheese**
> 2 **tablespoons chopped green chilies**
> 6 **flour tortillas**
> **Paprika**
> **Chili or taco sauce**

1. Preheat microwave browning grill for 5 minutes on HIGH.

2. Combine cheese and chilies. Divide mixture among tortillas. Fold tortillas in half, pressing edges together lightly.

3. Place tortillas on preheated grill.

4. Microwave for 45 seconds on HIGH. Turn tortillas over and continue cooking for 45 to 60 seconds, on HIGH, or until cheese is melted. Remove from grill and cool a few minutes. Sprinkle with paprika.

5. Cut each tortilla into 4 wedges. If desired, serve with chili or taco sauce.
                                                    24 Turnovers

TIP If tortillas are frozen, microwave for 45 to 60 seconds, on HIGH, or until easily separated.

PARMESAN NIBBLERS

    ¼ **cup butter or margarine**
    ½ **teaspoon garlic salt**
    4 **slices bread**
    ¼ **cup grated Parmesan cheese**

1. Microwave butter and garlic salt in small glass dish for about 45 seconds, on HIGH, or until melted. Stir to combine.

2. Remove crusts from bread. Brush both sides of each slice with butter mixture. Coat with cheese.

3. Preheat microwave browning grill for 4 minutes on HIGH.

4. Cut each bread slice into 5 strips. Spray surface of preheated grill with vegetable non-stick coating or grease lightly. Arrange strips on grill.

5. Microwave for 1 minute on HIGH. Turn strips over and continue cooking for 1 to 1½ minutes, on HIGH, or until crisp and lightly browned. Serve warm or cold.   20 Nibblers

Rinse tuna with water to remove excess oil.

TUNA TOASTWICHES

    1 **can (6½ oz.) tuna, drained**
    1 **cup shredded process American cheese**
    ⅓ **cup mayonnaise or salad dressing**
    ¼ **cup chopped sweet or dill pickle**
    2 **tablespoons chopped green onion**
    ½ **teaspoon prepared mustard**
    8 **slices bread**
    Sliced green olives

1. Combine tuna, cheese, mayonnaise, pickle, onion and mustard; mix well.

2. Trim crusts from bread; cut slices into quarters.

3. Preheat microwave browning grill for 4 minutes on HIGH.

4. Top bread pieces with tuna mixture; garnish with olives. Arrange half on preheated grill.

5. Microwave for 1 minute, on HIGH, or until cheese just starts to melt.

6. Reheat microwave browning grill for 2½ minutes on HIGH. Continue cooking remaining canapés as directed.   32 Canapés

CHEESE 'N BACON TOASTIES

    5 slices bacon
    ½ cup shredded Cheddar cheese
    2 tablespoons mayonnaise or salad dressing
    1 teaspoon caraway seed
    4 slices bread
    2 tablespoons butter or margarine

1. Arrange separated bacon slices in shallow glass baking dish.

2. Microwave for 4 to 4½ minutes, on HIGH, or until crisp. Crumble bacon into mixing bowl; add cheese, mayonnaise and caraway seed. Cut 2-inch circles from bread slices using a cookie or canapé cutter. Butter one side of bread circles; place buttered-side-down on tray or wax paper.

3. Preheat microwave browning grill for 4 minutes on HIGH.

4. Spoon 1 teaspoonful of bacon mixture onto each bread circle. Arrange circles on preheated grill.

5. Microwave for about 1 minute, on HIGH, or until cheese is melted.

About 16 Toasties

TOMATO TOPPER CANAPES

    4 slices bread
    1 tablespoon butter or margarine, softened
    1 package (3 oz.) cream cheese
    1 green onion, chopped
    ½ teaspoon prepared horseradish
    16 cherry tomatoes
    16 medium or 8 large canned smoked oysters

1. Remove crusts from bread; spread one side lightly with butter. Cut slices into quarters and place buttered-side-down on tray or wax paper.

2. Microwave cream cheese in small dish about 30 seconds, on HIGH, or until softened. Stir in onion and horseradish.

3. Divide cream cheese mixture among bread squares; spread mixture to cover bread.

4. Preheat microwave browning grill for 5 minutes on HIGH.

5. Turn tomatoes stem-side-down. Cut almost through each tomato twice to make petals. Spread apart tomato petals while arranging on each bread square. Place 1 medium or ½ large oyster in the center of each tomato. Arrange canapés on preheated grill.

6. Microwave for 1 to 1½ minutes, on HIGH, or until bread is toasted.

16 Canapés

TIP These can be assembled ahead of time and refrigerated. Then, just before serving, toast them on the preheated grill.

CHEESE MELTS

    ¼ **cup butter or margarine**
    2 **cups (8 oz.) shredded Cheddar cheese**
    1 **egg**
    ¼ **teaspoon salt**
    ¼ **teaspoon red pepper**
    ¼ **teaspoon paprika**
    ¼ **teaspoon Worcestershire sauce**
    11 **slices bread**

1. Microwave butter in glass mixing bowl for 20 to 30 seconds, on HIGH, or until softened. Blend in cheese, egg, salt, pepper, paprika and Worcestershire sauce; mix well.

2. Remove crusts from bread. Cut each slice into quarters.

3. Preheat microwave browning grill for 4 minutes on HIGH.

4. Top each bread square with a scant teaspoonful of cheese mixture. Arrange 15 squares on preheated grill.

5. Microwave for about 1 minute, on HIGH, or until cheese is melted.

6. Reheat microwave browning grill for 2½ minutes on HIGH. Continue cooking squares as directed. If desired, garnish with parsley.

44 Canapés

TIPS If desired, place a baby shrimp or cube of cooked ham on each bread square before adding topping.

● Mixture can be made up and refrigerated. For ease in spooning onto bread, allow cheese mixture to warm to room temperature or microwave about 15 seconds on HIGH.

● Some of cheese mixture may slide off of bread as it melts, but it can be easily spread on top of heated canapés.

MINI PIZZAS

    1 **can (8 oz.) refrigerated biscuits**
    ½ **cup tomato paste**
    ½ **teaspoon Italian seasoning**
    Pepperoni or other cooked meat
    ½ **cup shredded Mozzarella cheese**
    Parsley flakes

1. Separate biscuit dough into 10 biscuits. Divide each in half; flatten using a rolling pin or fingers. Combine tomato paste and Italian seasoning.

2. Preheat microwave browning grill for 4 minutes on HIGH.

3. Place half of flattened biscuits on preheated grill. Spread with half of tomato paste mixture; top with half of meat and cheese. Sprinkle with parsley.

4. Microwave for 1 to 1½ minutes, on HIGH, or until cheese melts.

5. Reheat microwave browning grill for 2 minutes on HIGH. Continue cooking remaining pizzas as directed.   20 Small Pizzas

With the use of the microwave browning grill, the frozen pizza rolls are super quick, yet have a crisp crust.

FROZEN PIZZA ROLLS

1. Preheat microwave browning grill for 5 minutes on HIGH.

2. Arrange 1 package (6 oz.) frozen pizza rolls on preheated grill.

3. Microwave for 1 minute on HIGH. Turn rolls over and continue cooking for 1½ to 2 minutes, on HIGH, or until lightly browned. Serve hot.   12 Rolls

Tasty, slightly crunchy mini wontons to make on your browning grill.

MICRO WONTONS

   1 can (4½ oz.) deviled ham
   1 tablespoon finely chopped green pepper
   ½ teaspoon dried parsley flakes
   4 egg roll or wonton skins (6 or 7-inch square size)
   Beaten egg

1. Combine ham, green pepper and parsley flakes; mix well.

2. Spread half of each egg roll skin with about 1 tablespoon filling. Roll up jelly-roll fashion starting with side that has filling. Moisten edge with water to seal to roll. Cover filled rolls with damp paper towel to prevent drying while filling other rolls.

3. Preheat microwave browning grill for 5 minutes on HIGH.

4. Brush rolls with beaten egg. Place seam-side-down on preheated grill.

5. Microwave for 1½ minutes on HIGH. Turn rolls over and continue cooking for 1 to 1½ minutes, on HIGH, or until heated. Cut each roll into 5 pieces.
                                                                20 Small Wontons

TIPS When using the 3 or 4-inch square skins, cut each in half.

● If skins are frozen, microwave 45 to 60 seconds or until they can be easily separated.

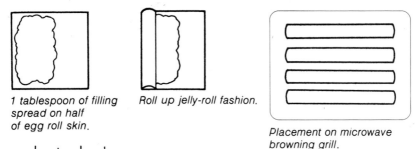

1 tablespoon of filling spread on half of egg roll skin.

Roll up jelly-roll fashion.

Placement on microwave browning grill.

Cut each roll in 5 equal parts.

main courses

And now to the heart of this menu matter — the main course. Even if it isn't strictly meat and potatoes, you can almost bet that the main course provides your family with the bulk of their daily protein and vitamin intake. Certainly nothing to be taken lightly by the cook or the critics!

If you're usually the "family chef", you will agree that it takes more than a little imagination and skill to avoid ho-hum dishes and not spend hours in the kitchen cooking up a little variety and dinner time excitement. And, even if a menu is chock-full of nutrients, we all know from experience that if it doesn't look good, it is apt to end up as an unwanted leftover.

To the rescue comes the microwave browning grill — with microwave speed and ease plus the ability to add that golden brown touch which makes grilled food an appetizing eyeful.

With a usual preheat time of 8 to 9 minutes (and a little less for high-sugar meats and precooked entrées), meats brown beautifully while you busy yourself preparing other dishes.

After experimenting, you will find that meats, such as steaks and chops, brown best if a little butter coats the grill surface.

You may use regular or lean ground meats with equal success. Browning is improved with a higher fat content, although the additional drippings are bound to spatter the inside of the oven a little more.

Egg and crumb coatings also brown nicely and offer a pleasant change from plain grilled meats. If the meat being coated is quite lean, you will want to grease the grill lightly for easier turning and clean-up.

What's in it for calorie and cholesterol watchers? A well around the browning surface serves to catch drippings from grilled meats, separating the unwanted fats from the food itself.

If you don't find your favorite meat timing in the recipes that follow, check the time chart on page 7.

Pictured: Crusty Fried Chicken, page 36.

PARMESAN BEEF PATTIES

    1 lb. ground beef
    1 egg
    ½ cup grated Parmesan cheese
    ¼ cup dry bread crumbs
    2 tablespoons catsup
    1 teaspoon dried parsley flakes
    ½ teaspoon garlic salt
    ¼ teaspoon leaf oregano
    Dash pepper

1. Preheat microwave browning grill for 8 minutes on HIGH.

2. Combine all ingredients; mix well. Shape into 4 patties about ½ inch thick. Place on preheated grill.

3. Microwave for 4 minutes on HIGH. Turn patties over and continue cooking for 3 to 4 minutes, on HIGH, or until desired doneness.   4 Servings

Use same cooking times for plain hamburger patties.

GLORIFIED HAMBURGER PATTIES

    1½ lbs. ground beef
    2 slices bread, crumbled
    ⅓ cup milk
    ¼ cup chopped onion
    ¼ cup catsup
    2 tablespoons chopped green pepper
    1 teaspoon salt
    2 teaspoons Worcestershire sauce
    ½ teaspoon dry mustard
    ¼ teaspoon pepper

1. Preheat microwave browning grill on HIGH for 8 minutes.

2. Combine all ingredients; mix well. Shape into 6 patties, about ½ inch thick. Place on preheated grill.

3. Microwave for 4 minutes on HIGH. Turn patties over and continue cooking for 5 to 6 minutes, on HIGH, or until desired doneness.   6 Servings

SWISS MINUTE STEAKS

    4 minute steaks (about 4 ozs. each)
    1 small onion, sliced
    1 can (8 oz.) tomato sauce
    ½ teaspoon garlic salt
    2 teaspoons dried parsley flakes

1. Preheat microwave browning grill for 8 minutes on HIGH.

2. Arrange steaks on preheated grill; place onion at edge of grill.

3. Microwave for 4 minutes on HIGH. Turn steaks over and continue cooking for 4 to 5 minutes, on HIGH, or until desired doneness.

4. Place steaks on serving plate. Combine partially cooked onion slices and remaining ingredients in 2-cup glass measure.

5. Microwave for 1½ to 2 minutes, on HIGH, or until bubbly. Pour over steaks. If desired, garnish with additional parsley.   4 Servings

SWEET-SOUR MEATBALLS

1½ **tablespoons cornstarch**
⅓ **cup packed brown sugar**
1 **can (15¼ oz.) chunk pineapple, undrained**
1 **tablespoon soy sauce**
¼ **cup vinegar**
¼ **cup chopped green pepper**
1 **lb. ground beef**
1 **egg**
¼ **cup chopped onion**
2 **slices bread, crumbled**
¼ **cup milk**
¾ **teaspoon salt**
⅛ **teaspoon pepper**
1 **teaspoon Worcestershire sauce**

1. Combine cornstarch, brown sugar, pineapple, soy sauce, vinegar and green pepper in 4-cup glass measure.

2. Microwave for 3 minutes on HIGH. Stir and continue cooking for 2 to 3 minutes, on HIGH, or until sauce boils and thickens. Set aside.

3. Combine ground beef and remaining ingredients; mix well.

4. Preheat microwave browning grill for 8 minutes on HIGH.

5. Shape meat mixture into about 12 meatballs. Place on preheated grill.

6. Microwave for 2 minutes on HIGH. Turn meatballs over and continue cooking for 2 minutes on HIGH. Turn meatballs again and continue cooking for 1½ to 2½ minutes, on HIGH, or until desired doneness. Place meatballs in glass serving dish or 1½-quart casserole. Spoon sweel-sour sauce over meatballs.

7. Microwave for 2 to 2½ minutes, on HIGH, or until heated.

4 to 5 Servings

Marinating and medium-rare doneness assure tender eating.

TERIYAKI STEAK

½ **cup soy sauce**
2 **tablespoons honey**
1 **tablespoon vinegar**
½ **teaspoon ground ginger**
1 **clove garlic, finely chopped**
1½-**lb. beef flank steak**
1 **tablespoon butter or margarine**

1. Combine all ingredients except steak and butter in shallow glass baking dish. Add steak, turning to coat with marinade. Cover and allow to marinate in refrigerator at least 6 hours or overnight.

2. Preheat microwave browning grill for 8 minutes on HIGH.

3. Remove steak from marinade; drain excess liquid. Coat preheated grill with butter. Place steak on grill.

4. Microwave for 3 minutes on HIGH. Turn steak over and continue cooking for 3 to 4 minutes, on HIGH, or until desired doneness. To serve, carve meat across grain into thin slices.　　　　　4 to 6 Servings

Remove from grill immediately to avoid overcooking.

FILETS MIGNONS WITH BUTTER-MUSTARD SAUCE

½ **cup butter or margarine**
1½ **teaspoons Dijon-style mustard**
1½ **teaspoons Worcestershire sauce**
⅛ **teaspoon pepper**
4 **beef filets mignons (4 to 6 ozs. each)**
Salt

1. Microwave butter in glass dish for 20 to 30 seconds, on HIGH, or until softened. Beat in mustard, Worcestershire sauce and pepper. Let stand at room temperature.

2. Preheat microwave browning grill for 9 minutes.

3. Dip one side of each filet into seasoned butter. Place filets buttered-side-down on preheated grill.

4. Microwave for 5 minutes on HIGH. Turn filets over and continue cooking for 4 to 5 minutes; on HIGH, or until desired doneness. Season with salt; serve with Butter-Mustard Sauce.   4 Servings

TIP For bacon-wrapped filets, wrap a partially cooked slice of bacon around each filet, fastening with toothpicks. Cook as directed above. If sauce is omitted, spread a little butter on filets before cooking.

"MOCK" FILETS

1½ **lb. beef flank steak**
½ **cup cooking oil**
¼ **cup lemon juice**
1 **teaspoon instant minced onion**
8 **whole peppercorns, crushed**
4 **slices bacon**

1. Score steak diagonally in diamond-shape cuts about 1 inch apart and ¼ inch deep. Cut steak lenghwise into 4 strips.

2. Combine oil, lemon juice, onion and peppercorns in shallow bowl. Add the meat, turning to coat evenly with marinade. Cover and refrigerate at least 6 hours, turning once or twice.

3. Preheat microwave browning grill for 4 minutes on HIGH. Place bacon on preheated grill.

4. Microwave for 2 minutes on HIGH. Remove bacon; drain drippings from well.

5. Reheat microwave browning grill for 3 minutes on HIGH. Roll steak strips jelly-roll fashion. Wrap each with a bacon strip, securing with toothpicks. Place steaks on preheated grill.

6. Microwave for 3 minutes on HIGH. Turn steaks over and continue cooking for 3 to 4 minutes, on HIGH, or until desired doneness.   4 Servings

T-BONES WITH MUSHROOM SAUCE

> **1 can (2 oz.) mushroom stems and pieces, drained**
> **½ can (10¾-oz. size) condensed cream of mushroom soup**
> **1 tablespoon dry sherry**
> **2 tablespoons sour cream**
> **½ tablespoon dried parsley flakes**
> **1 tablespoon butter or margarine**
> **2 T-bone steaks (8 ozs. each)**

1. Prepare Mushroom Sauce by combining drained mushrooms, soup and sherry in 4-cup glass measure.

2. Microwave for 2 to 3 minutes, on HIGH, or until bubbly. Stir in sour cream and parsley; set aside.

3. Preheat microwave browning grill for 9 minutes on HIGH.

4. Coat preheated grill with butter. Place steaks on grill.

5. Microwave for 5 minutes on HIGH. Turn steaks over and continue cooking for 1 to 2 minutes, on HIGH, or until desired doneness.

6. Microwave sauce for 1 minute, on HIGH, or until heated. Serve over steaks.   2 Large Servings

Butter adds flavor and improves browning.

SIRLOIN AU POIVRE

> **2 lb. sirloin steak, cut 1-inch thick**
> **1 teaspoon whole peppercorns**
> **1 tablespoon butter or margarine**
> **2 tablespoons brandy**
> **Salt**

1. Preheat microwave browning grill for 9 minutes on HIGH.

2. Place peppercorns between layers of wax paper. Crush with rollin pin. Press crushed peppercorns into both sides of steak.

3. Coat preheated grill with butter. Place steak on grill.

4. Microwave for 5 minutes on HIGH. Turn steak over and continue cooking for 1 to 2 minutes, on HIGH, or until desired doneness. Place steak on serving platter.

5. Pour brandy on grill; mix with drippings. Pour over steak on serving plate. Cut into serving pieces.   4 to 6 Servings

GRILLED FAMILY STEAK

1. Sprinkle a 2½ to 3-lb. family steak (about 1½ inches thick) with meat tenderizer as directed on tenderizer label.

2. Preheat microwave browning grill for 9 minutes on HIGH.

3. Coat preheated grill with about ½ tablespoon butter or margarine. Place steak on grill.

4. Microwave for 6 minutes on HIGH. Turn steak over and continue cooking for 6 to 8 minutes, on HIGH, or until steak is a medium-rare doneness. Carve meat into thin slices for serving.   6 to 8 Servings

Coatings on meats brown well and help seal in juices.

BREADED SMOKED CHOPS

  ½ **cup dry bread crumbs**
  ¼ **teaspoon ground thyme**
  ⅓ **cup crushed French-fried onion rings**
  1 **egg, beaten**
  1 **tablespoon water**
  4 **smoked pork chops, cut ½-inch thick**

1. Preheat microwave browning grill for 8 minutes on HIGH.

2. Combine crumbs, thyme and onion on wax paper. Beat together egg and water in shallow bowl.

3. Dip chops into egg mixture; coat with crumb mixture. Place on preheated grill.

4. Microwave on HIGH for 6 minutes. Turn chops over and continue cooking on HIGH for 6 to 7 minutes or until desired doneness.   4 Servings

Pork requires longer cooking for fork tenderness.

ZIPPY BARBECUED CHOPS

  ¼ **cup catsup**
  ¼ **cup chili sauce**
  1 **tablespoon brown sugar**
  2 **tablespoons chopped onion**
  ½ **teaspoon salt**
  ⅛ **teaspoon garlic powder**
  1 **teaspoon dry mustard**
  2 **teaspoons Worcestershire sauce**
    Dash Tabasco sauce
  1 **tablespoon lemon juice**
  4 **rib or loin pork chops, cut ½-inch thick**

1. Combine all ingredients except chops in 2-cup glass measure.

2. Microwave for 1 to 1½ minutes, on HIGH, or until bubbly.

3. Preheat microwave browning grill for 8 minutes on HIGH.

4. Place chops on preheated grill.

5. Microwave for 9 minutes on HIGH. Turn chops over and continue cooking for 6 minutes on HIGH. Spoon sauce over chops and cook for 4 to 6 minutes, on HIGH, or until chops are fork tender.   4 Servings

Note the shorter preheat time for cooked ham – browns without drying slices.

HAM SLICES WITH ORANGE SAUCE

¼ **cup packed brown sugar**
2 **tablespoons honey or light corn syrup**
2 **teaspoons grated orange peel**
½ **cup orange juice**
1 **tablespoon cornstarch**
1 **to 1½ lbs. ready-to-eat ham, sliced ½-inch thick**

1. Combine brown sugar, honey, orange peel and juice and cornstarch in 4-cup glass measure.

2. Microwave for 1½ minutes on HIGH. Stir mixture and continue cooking for 1 to 1½ minutes, on HIGH, or until mixture boils.

3. Preheat microwave browning grill for 7 minutes on HIGH. Place ham slices on preheated grill.

4. Microwave for 1½ minutes on HIGH. Turn slices over and continue cooking for 1 to 2 minutes, on HIGH, or until heated. Serve sauce over slices.

4 to 6 Servings

Veal should be pounded very thin.

WIENER SCHNITZEL

1 **lb. boneless veal round steak, cut into serving pieces**
2 **eggs**
2 **tablespoons water**
2 **tablespoons cooking oil**
1 **tablespoon lemon juice**
1 **teaspoon salt**
¼ **teaspoon pepper**
1 **cup dry bread crumbs**
⅔ **cup grated Parmesan cheese**

1. Place pieces of veal between layers of plastic wrap and pound with flat side of meat mallet or rolling pin until ¼-inch thick.

2. Beat together eggs, water, oil, lemon juice, salt and pepper in shallow bowl. Combine bread crumbs and Parmesan cheese on wax paper. Dip veal into egg mixture, allowing excess to drain off. Coat each with bread crumb mixture. Dip again into egg and coat with crumbs. Let stand about 15 minutes to dry coating.

3. Preheat microwave browning grill for 8 minutes on HIGH.

4. Spray surface of preheated grill with vegetable non-stick coating or grease lightly. Place a layer of cutlets on grill.

5. Microwave for 2 minutes on HIGH. Turn cutlets over and continue cooking for 2½ to 3½ minutes, on HIGH, or until lightly browned and tender.

6. Scrape off grill surface; reheat microwave browning grill for 5 minutes on HIGH. Grease grill and continue cooking remaining cutlets as directed.

4 to 5 Servings

TIP Pork can be substituted for veal. Use pieces of tenderloin, flattening as directed.

Since veal contains little fat, grill surface needs greasing to prevent crumb coating from sticking.

VEAL PARMIGIANA

⅓ **cup grated Parmesan cheese**
2 **tablespoons dry bread crumbs**
1 **egg, slightly beaten**
1 **to 1½ lbs. veal cutlets or boneless round steak, cut ½-inch thick**
2 **tablespoons chopped onion**
4 **ozs. sliced or shredded Mozzarella cheese**
1 **can (8 oz.) tomato sauce**
½ **teaspoon salt**
⅛ **teaspoon pepper**
¼ **teaspoon Italian seasoning**
Parmesan cheese

1. Preheat microwave browning grill for 8 minutes on HIGH.

2. Combine Parmesan cheese and bread crumbs on wax paper. Beat egg in shallow bowl. Cut veal into serving pieces. Dip veal pieces in egg; coat with crumbs.

3. Spray surface of preheated grill with non-stick vegetable coating or grease lightly. Place coated veal on grill; add chopped onion at edge of grill.

4. Microwave for 2 minutes on HIGH. Turn veal pieces over and continue cooking for 2½ to 3½ minutes, on HIGH, or until tender.

5. Place veal and onions in shallow 1½-quart glass casserole. Top with cheese, tomato sauce, salt, pepper and Italian seasoning. Cover with glass lid or wax paper.

6. Microwave for 5 to 6 minutes, on HIGH, or until bubbly. Sprinkle with Parmesan cheese. Continue cooking for 1 minute on HIGH.

4 to 6 Servings

To prevent excessive spattering, select fairly lean meat.

ORANGE-SPARKED LAMB PATTIES

1½ **lbs. ground lamb**
¼ **cup dry bread crumbs**
¼ **cup orange juice**
1 **egg**
½ **teaspoon grated orange peel**
½ **teaspoon salt**
1 **teaspoon leaf marjoram**
1 **tablespoon Worcestershire sauce**

1. Combine all ingredients; mix well.

2. Preheat microwave browning grill for 8 minutes on HIGH.

3 Shape meat mixture into 6 patties, about ½ inch thick. Place patties on preheated grill.

4. Microwave for 2½ minutes on HIGH. Turn patties over and continue cooking for 2 to 3 minutes, on HIGH, or until desired doneness.

6 Servings

Trim excess fat from chops before grilling.

GRILLED LAMB CHOPS

> 6 **rib lamb chops, cut 1-inch thick**
> ¼ **cup cooking oil**
> 3 **tablespoons chopped stuffed green olives**
> 2 **tablespoons lemon juice**
> 1 **clove garlic, finely chopped**
> ½ **teaspoon salt**
> ¼ **teaspoon leaf marjoram**
> ¼ **teaspoon leaf basil**
> ⅛ **teaspoon pepper**

1. Place chops in 8 to 9-inch shallow round glass dish. Combine remaining ingredients; pour over chops. Cover and allow to marinate in refrigerator for 2 to 3 hours, turning chops over once.

2. Preheat microwave browning grill for 8 minutes on HIGH.

3. Remove chops from marinade; drain excess liquid. Place chops on pre-heated grill.

4. Microwave for 8 minutes on HIGH. Turn chops over; spoon some of marinade over chops. Continue cooking for 7 to 8 minutes, on HIGH, or until desired doneness.   About 6 Servings

Start 1 hour ahead so the meat can marinate.

LAMB KABOBS

> 1 **lb. lean boneless lamb, cut into 1-inch cubes**
> 8 **to 12 cherry tomatoes**
> 8 **to 12 fresh mushrooms**
> 4 **wooden skewers (8-inch size)**
> ½ **cup French salad dressing**

1. Thread lamb, tomatoes and mushrooms alternately on wooden skewers, beginning and ending with lamb. Place kabobs in shallow dish. Pour French dressing over kabobs, coating meat and vegetables. Cover and allow to marinate in dressing at least 1 hour.

2. Preheat microwave browning grill for 8 minutes on HIGH.

3. Remove kabobs from marinade; allow excess dressing to drain off. Place kabobs on preheated grill.

4. Microwave for 2 minutes on HIGH; turn each kabob over and continue cooking for 3 to 4 minutes, on HIGH, or until meat is desired doneness.
                                         4 Servings

TIPS One medium zucchini, cut into ¼-inch slices can be substituted for mushrooms.

• Vegetables should be slightly smaller in diameter than meat cubes so the meat will rest on grill and brown.

WIENERS

1. Preheat microwave browning grill for 8 minutes on HIGH.

2. Place 10 wieners on preheated grill.

3. Microwave for 1 minute on HIGH. Turn wieners over and continue cooking for 1 to 1½ minutes, on HIGH, or until heated. 10 Wieners

CANADIAN BACON

1. Preheat microwave browning grill for 8 minutes on HIGH.

2. Place 6 slices Canadian-style bacon, cut ¼-inch thick, on preheated grill.

3. Microwave for 1½ minutes on HIGH. Turn bacon over and continue cooking for 1½ to 2 minutes, on HIGH, or until heated. 6 Servings

SAUSAGE LINKS

1. Preheat microwave browning grill for 8 minutes on HIGH.

2. Arrange 12 link sausages on preheated grill.

3. Microwave for 1 minute on HIGH. Turn sausages over and continue cooking for 1½ minutes on HIGH. Turn sausages again and cook for 1 to 1½ minutes, on HIGH, or until done. 4 to 6 Servings

SAUSAGE PATTIES

1. Preheat microwave browning grill for 8 minutes on HIGH.

2. Cut 12-oz. package of sausage into 10 slices. Place slices on preheated grill.

3. Microwave for 1½ minutes on HIGH. Turn patties over and continue cooking for 2½ to 3½ minutes, on HIGH, or until done.

About 5 Servings

BRATWURST

1. Preheat microwave browning grill for 8 minutes on HIGH.

2. Place 1 lb. uncooked bratwurst on preheated grill.

3. Microwave for 3 minutes on HIGH. Turn bratwurst over and continue cooking for 4 to 5 minutes, on HIGH, or until done. 5 to 6 Servings

Already-cooked sausages only need to heat.

GRILLED KNACKWURST

> **1 small onion, chopped**
> **2 tablespoons butter or margarine**
> **¼ teaspoon caraway seed**
> **½ teaspoon prepared mustard**
> **8 knackwurst sausages**

1. Combine onion and butter in small glass dish.

2. Microwave for 4 to 5 minutes on HIGH, or until tender. Stir in caraway and mustard.

3. Preheat microwave browning grill for 8 minutes on HIGH. Arrange sausages on preheated grill.

4. Microwave for 3 minutes on HIGH. Turn sausages over. Make a slit down length of sausage, cutting almost through and to within ½ inch of each end. Open slit enough to spoon some of onion mixture into each sausage. Continue cooking for 2 to 3 minutes, on HIGH, or until heated.

6 to 8 Servings

TIP Catsup can be substituted for mustard. Use 1 to 2 tablespoons.

Baby beef liver is more tender, but regular beef liver can also be used successfully if not overcooked.

LIVER, BACON AND ONIONS

> **4 slices bacon**
> **2 medium onions, sliced**
> **1 lb. beef liver, sliced and cut into serving pieces**

1. Preheat microwave browning grill for 4 minutes on HIGH. Place bacon and onion slices on preheated grill.

2. Microwave for 2 to 3 minutes, on HIGH, or until partially cooked. Push bacon and onions to edge of grill and into drippings.

3. Reheat microwave browning grill for 6 minutes on HIGH. Place liver on preheated grill.

4. Microwave for 3 minutes on HIGH. Turn liver over and continue cooking for 3 to 4 minutes, on HIGH, or until no longer pink. Serve liver topped with onions and bacon.

4 to 6 Servings

Keep larger, thicker parts of chicken pieces toward outside of grill.

CRUSTY FRIED CHICKEN

> 1 **cup cornflake crumbs**
> 2 **tablespoons dried parsley flakes**
> 1 **teaspoon salt**
> ¼ **teaspoon poultry seasoning**
> ⅛ **teaspoon pepper**
> 1 **egg, beaten**
> 2 **tablespoons water**
> 2½ **to 3-lb. frying chicken, quartered**

1. Combine crumbs, parsley, salt, poultry seasoning and pepper on wax paper or in plastic bag. Combine egg and water in shallow bowl.

2. Preheat microwave browning grill for 8 minutes on HIGH.

3. Dip chicken quarters into egg mixture; coat with cornflake mixture. Place skin-side-down on preheated grill.

4. Microwave for 10 minutes on HIGH. Turn chicken over and continue cooking for 15 to 17 minutes, on HIGH, or until chicken is fork tender.

About 4 Servings

Take time to seal edges carefully so cheese will not cook out.

CHICKEN CORDON BLEU

> 4 **whole chicken breasts, halved, skinned and boned**
> **Salt**
> 4 **ounces Swiss cheese**
> 4 **slices boiled ham**
> 1 **egg, beaten**
> 3 **tablespoons water**
> ⅓ **cup unsifted all-purpose flour**
> ¾ **cup dry bread crumbs**

1. Place chicken breasts, one at a time, between sheets of plastic wrap. Using the flat side of meat mallet or rolling pin, pound to ¼-inch thickness. Sprinkle each with salt.

2. Cut cheese into 8 sticks, each about 1 inch long. Cut ham slices in half. Roll up cheese stick inside of each ham slice. Place a ham-cheese roll on boned side of each chicken breast. Roll up jelly-roll fashion, tucking in ends to seal cheese inside. Fasten with toothpicks.

3. Preheat microwave browning grill for 8 minutes on HIGH.

4. Beat together egg and water in shallow bowl. Coat each chicken breast with flour; dip into egg mixture; coat with bread crumbs. Place seam-side-up on preheated grill.

5. Microwave for 5 minutes on HIGH. Turn rolls over and continue cooking for 5 to 6 minutes, on HIGH, or until chicken is done. *About 8 Servings*

Precooked ingredients require heating only.

MEXICAN BEAN CAKES

> 1 **can (15 oz.) pinto beans, drained**
> 2 **tablespoons chopped onion**
> 2 **tablespoons chopped green chilies**
> ½ **teaspoon ground thyme**
> ½ **cup cubed cooked ham**
> ½ **cup shredded Monterey Jack cheese**
> ⅓ **cup grated Parmesan cheese**
> 1 **egg, beaten**
> 2 **tablespoons all-purpose flour**
> ½ **cup yellow cornmeal**

1. Mash beans thoroughly. Stir in onion, chilies, thyme, ham and cheeses. Shape into 4 patties.

2. Preheat microwave browning grill for 8 minutes on HIGH.

3. Beat egg in shallow bowl or pie pan. Coat patties with flour; dip into beaten egg and coat with cornmeal. Place on preheated grill.

4. Microwave for 2 minutes on HIGH. Turn patties over and continue cooking for 1 to 2 minutes, on HIGH, or until heated.   4 Servings

Patties are easier to shape if macaroni mixture is chilled first.

TUNA AND MACARONI CROQUETTES

> 1 **package (7¼ oz.) macaroni and cheese dinner mix**
> 1 **can (10¾ oz.) condensed cream of celery soup**
> 1 **cup water**
> 1 **teaspoon dried parsley flakes**
> 1 **can (6½ oz.) tuna, drained**
> ¼ **cup chopped green pepper**
> 1 **cup dry bread crumbs**

1. Combine uncooked macaroni, soup and water in 2-quart glass casserole. Cover with glass lid.

2. Microwave for 6 minutes on HIGH. Stir mixture and continue cooking for 4 to 5 minutes, on HIGH, or until macaroni is tender. Cool.

3. Stir in parsley, tuna, green pepper, cheese from mix and ½ cup of the bread crumbs. Chill.

4. Preheat microwave browning grill for 8 minutes on HIGH. Form chilled macaroni mixture into 6 patties; coat with remaining ½ cup bread crumbs. Place on preheated grill.

5. Microwave for 4 minutes on HIGH. Turn patties over and continue cooking for 4 to 5 minutes, on HIGH, or until heated and lightly toasted.6 Servings

TIP Mixture may seem a little sticky for shaping into patties, but chilling and coating with crumbs will make the forming easier.

Remove from grill immediately so fish does not overcook.

FILLET OF SOLE ROLLS

  2 tablespoons butter or margarine
  2 tablespoons lemon juice
  1 teaspoon dried parsley flakes
  1 teaspoon anchovy paste
  ¼ teaspoon salt
  1 to 1½ lbs. sole fillets
  1 can (4 oz.) whole mushrooms, drained
  Paprika

1. Combine butter, lemon juice, parsley, anchovy paste and salt in 1-cup glass measure.

2. Microwave for 45 to 60 seconds, on HIGH, or until butter is melted.

3. Preheat microwave browning grill for 8 minutes on HIGH.

4. Cut sole fillets into ¾ to 1-inch wide strips, making the same number of strips as there are mushrooms. Place a mushroom at end of each strip. Roll up each with a mushroom inside; fasten each with toothpick. Dip rolls in butter sauce; place on preheated grill. Sprinkle with paprika.

5. Microwave for 1½ minutes on HIGH. Turn rolls over and continue cooking for 1 to 2 minutes, on HIGH, or until fish flakes easily. Serve remaining sauce over rolls.   4 to 6 Servings

CHEESY CAESAR FISH FILLETS

  1½ lbs. fish fillets, cut into serving pieces
  ½ cup Caesar salad dressing
  ¾ cup dry bread crumbs
  1 tablespoon dried parsley flakes
  ½ cup shredded Cheddar cheese

1. Preheat microwave browning grill for 8 minutes on HIGH.

2. Pat fish dry with paper towels. Dip fish into salad dressing; coat with mixture of bread crumbs and parsley.

3. Spray surface of preheated grill with vegetable non-stick coating or grease lightly. Place fillets on grill.

4. Microwave for 2 minutes on HIGH. Turn fillets over and top with cheese. Continue cooking for 1½ to 2 minutes, on HIGH, or until fish flakes easily.
                                              5 to 6 Servings

Direct narrow ends toward center of grill where they cook more slowly.

SESAME SALMON STEAKS

> ½ **cup butter or margarine**
> ½ **teaspoon garlic salt**
> 4 **salmon steaks, cut ¾-inch thick**
> ½ **cup (2¼-oz. package) sesame seed**
> 1½ **tablespoons lemon juice**
> ½ **teaspoon dill weed**

1. Microwave butter in 1-cup glass measure for 45 to 60 seconds, on HIGH, or until melted. Stir in garlic salt.

2. Preheat microwave browning grill for 8 minutes on HIGH.

3. Brush salmon steaks with butter mixture. Coat with sesame seed. Place on preheated grill.

4. Microwave for 2½ minutes on HIGH. Turn steaks over and continue cooking for 3 to 3½ minutes, on HIGH, or until fish flakes easily. Add lemon juice and dill weed to remaining butter mixture.

5. Microwave for 15 to 30 seconds, on HIGH, or until hot. Serve with salmon.

4 Servings

FISH STICKS

1. Preheat microwave browning grill for 7 minutes on HIGH.

2. Spray surface of preheated grill with vegetable non-stick coating or grease lightly. Arrange about 8 frozen fish sticks (half a 1-lb. pkg.) on grill.

3. Microwave for 2 minutes on HIGH. Turn sticks over and continue cooking for 1½ to 2 minutes, on HIGH, or until heated.

4. Reheat microwave browning grill for 5 minutes on HIGH. Continue cooking remaining fish sticks as directed. 4 to 5 Servings

BREADED FISH PORTIONS

1. Preheat microwave browning grill for 7 minutes on HIGH.

2. Spray surface of preheated grill with vegetable non-stick coating or grease lightly. Arrange half a 2-lb. package frozen breaded fish portions on grill.

3. Microwave for 3 minutes on HIGH. Turn portions over and continue cooking for 2 to 3 minutes, on HIGH, or until heated.

4. Reheat microwave browning grill for 5 minutes on HIGH. Continue cooking remaining portions as directed. 8 to 10 Servings

sandwiches **& breads**

A new lease on lunch or snack time is yours with this tempting array of hot sandwich and bread ideas and a microwave browning grill at your fingertips.

The versatility and speed of your grill should help you beat those peanut butter and jelly blues — and won't your family be happy about that?

With just a 5-minute preheat time, sandwiches and breads brown readily and evenly. Sandwiches which need browning on both sides are turned half way through the cooking time. And, since the grill begins to cool as soon as food is placed upon the surface, the sooner the sandwiches are turned, the more heat is available for toasting the second side.

You will be expert in the breads department in no time if you remember one thing — all types overcook easily. Whether you begin with do-it-yourself dough or start with the ready-baked variety, allow breads to remain on the grill until barely hot. Again, a 5-minute preheat time is required.

And for pizza fans, at last a crisp crust that is pizza parlor proud. The hot grill surface works wonders to combat crust sogginess.

Although most of our recipes utilize the entire grill area, the adjustment to smaller quantities is a snap. Just use the same 5-minute preheat time, but decrease the microwave cooking time proportionately to the decrease in quantity.

Pictured: Grilled Cheese Sandwiches, page 42.

GRILLED REUBENS

> **8 slices rye or pumpernickel bread**
> **3 ounces sliced cooked corned beef**
> **¾ cup well-drained sauerkraut**
> **2 tablespoons Thousand Island dressing**
> **4 slices Swiss cheese**
> **2 tablespoons butter or margarine, softened**

1. Top half of bread slices with corned beef. Combine sauerkraut and salad dressing. Spread over corned beef. Top with cheese slices and remaining bread slices.

2. Preheat microwave browning grill for 5 minutes on HIGH.

3. Spread outside of sandwiches with butter. Arrange on preheated grill.

4. Microwave for 30 seconds on HIGH. Turn sandwiches over and continue cooking for 1 to 1½ minutes, on HIGH, or until filling is hot.   4 Reubens

GRILLED CHEESE SANDWICHES

> **8 slices bread**
> **4 slices cheese**
> **¼ cup butter or margarine, softened**

1. Preheat microwave browning grill for 5 minutes on HIGH.

2. Top half of bread slices with cheese slices, then with remaining bread slices. Spread outside of sandwiches with butter. Place on preheated grill.

3. Microwave for 1 minute on HIGH. Turn sandwiches over and continue cooking for 1 to 1½ minutes, on HIGH, or until cheese is melted. Allow to stand on grill a few minutes to finish toasting.   4 Sandwiches

TIP For 2 sandwiches, prepare as directed, but microwave on second side 30 to 45 seconds.

OPEN-FACED CHEESE 'N TOMATO SANDWICHES

> **4 slices bread**
> **Mayonnaise or salad dressing**
> **2 tomatoes, sliced ½-inch thick**
> **4 slices Cheddar, Swiss or American cheese**

1. Preheat microwave browning grill for 5 minutes on HIGH.

2. Place bread slices on preheated grill.

3. Microwave for 1 minute on HIGH. Turn bread slices over; spread each slice with mayonnaise. Top with tomato and cheese slices.

4. Microwave for 1½ to 2 minutes, on HIGH, or until cheese is melted.
                                          4 Sandwiches

Hamburger buns are toasted on the hot grill before being topped with a tasty sandwich spread.

BOLOGNA BURGERS

½ cup ground or finely chopped bologna
½ cup shredded Cheddar cheese
1 tablespoon finely chopped onion
1 tablespoon chopped pickle
1 tablespoon mayonnaise or salad dressing
3 hamburger buns, split
1 tablespoon butter or margarine, softened

1. Combine bologna, cheese, onion, pickle, and mayonnaise; set aside.

2. Preheat microwave browning grill for 5 minutes on HIGH.

3. Spread cut sides of buns with butter. Arrange buns, buttered-side-down, on preheated grill.

4. Microwave for 30 seconds on HIGH. Turn buns over; top with bologna mixture.

5. Microwave for 1½ to 2 minutes, on HIGH, or until cheese is melted.

6 Small Sandwiches

TIP Use this idea of toasting buns on browning grill for other similar sandwiches.

The grill adds a golden brown color to the biscuit wrappers.

WIENERS IN BLANKETS

1 can (8 oz.) refrigerated biscuits
Mustard or catsup
5 wieners
2 tablespoons butter or margarine
Sesame or poppy seed, if desired

1. Separate biscuit dough into 10 biscuits. Flatten each to oval about 3 inches long. Spread surface with mustard or catsup to within ½ inch of edge. Cut wieners in half crosswise. Place one piece on each biscuit. Wrap biscuit around wieners, sealing edges by pinching together.

2. Microwave butter in small dish for 30 seconds, on HIGH, or until melted.

3. Preheat microwave browning grill for 5 minutes on HIGH.

4. Dip wrapped wieners in butter to coat all sides; sprinkle with seeds. Arrange on preheated grill.

5. Microwave for 30 seconds on HIGH. Turn biscuits over and continue cooking for 2 to 2½ minutes, on HIGH, or until biscuits are done.

10 Small Sandwiches

OPEN-FACED HAMBURGERS

    8 slices bread
    Mustard
    1 lb. lean ground beef
    1 small onion, chopped
    1 teaspoon salt
    ¼ teaspoon pepper
    Catsup or barbecue sauce

1. Spread one side of bread slices with mustard. Combine beef, onion, salt and pepper.

2. Preheat microwave browning grill for 4 minutes on HIGH.

3. Divide meat mixture into eight portions; flatten each to size of bread. Place a patty on each bread slice. Brush meat with catsup. Arrange 4 slices, meat-side-up, on preheated grill.

4. Microwave for 4 to 5 minutes, on HIGH, or until meat is done.

5. Reheat microwave browning grill for 2 minutes on HIGH. Continue cooking remaining sandwiches as directed.   8 Sandwiches

Now you can prepare frozen pizza in the microwave and still have a crisp crust.

FROZEN PIZZA

1. Preheat microwave browning grill for 5 minutes on HIGH.

2. Place 10-inch frozen pizza on preheated grill.

3. Microwave for 5 to 6 minutes, on HIGH, or until cheese is bubbly near center of pizza.   1 Pizza

Use this idea for turning an ordinary frozen pizza into your own special creation.

DELUXE FROZEN PIZZA

    10-inch frozen cheese pizza
    ¼ cup chopped green pepper
    ¼ cup sliced green olives
    1 jar (2½ oz.) sliced mushrooms, drained
    ¼ cup shredded Mozzarella cheese

1. Preheat microwave browning grill for 5 minutes on HIGH.

2. Remove wrap from pizza and top with remaining ingredients. Place pizza on preheated grill.

3. Microwave for 6 to 7 minutes, on HIGH, or until cheese is bubbly near center of pizza.   1 Pizza

BRUNCH MUFFINS

   4 **eggs**
   ¼ **cup milk**
   ¼ **teaspoon salt**
   1 **tablespoon butter or margarine**
   2 **English muffins, split**
   2 **tablespoons butter or margarine, softened**
   4 **slices process American cheese**

1. Beat together eggs, milk and salt in 1-quart glass casserole; add butter. Cover with glass lid.

2. Microwave for 2 minutes on HIGH. Stir lightly and continue cooking for 30 to 60 seconds, on HIGH, or until just about set. Set aside.

3. Preheat microwave browning grill for 5 minutes on HIGH.

4. Spread cut side of English muffins with butter. Arrange muffins, cut-side-down, on preheated grill.

5. Microwave for 1 minute, on HIGH, or until toasted. Turn muffins over and top each with scrambled eggs and a slice of cheese.

6. Microwave for 45 to 60 seconds, on HIGH, or until heated.   4 Muffins

TIP Thin slices ham or corned beef can be placed on muffins before topping with eggs.

SOUR CREAM SCONES

   2 **cups unsifted all-purpose flour**
   2 **tablespoons sugar**
   3 **teaspoons baking powder**
   1 **teaspoon salt**
   ¼ **teaspoon soda**
   ¼ **cup shortening**
   ½ **cup raisins**
   ¼ **cup milk**
   ½ **cup sour cream**
   1 **egg, slightly beaten**

1. Combine flour, sugar, baking powder, salt and soda. Cut in shortening until crumbly. Stir in raisins, milk, sour cream and egg until just moistened.

2. Preheat microwave browning grill for 4 minutes on HIGH.

3. Turn dough onto floured surface and knead 10 to 12 times. Divide dough in half. Pat each half into a 6-inch circle with a slightly rounded top. Cut each circle into 6 wedges. Place 6 wedges 1 inch apart on preheated grill with top-side-down and points toward center of grill.

4. Microwave for 2 minutes on HIGH. Turn scones over and continue cooking for 1 to 1½ minutes, on HIGH, or until sides are dry to the touch.

5. Reheat microwave browning grill for 2½ minutes on HIGH. Continue cooking remaining scones as directed. Serve warm with butter and jam.
                                                                12 Scones

TIP For a surprise cinnamon filling, split each scone before cooking and sprinkle with a mixture of 2 tablespoons sugar and 2 teaspoons cinnamon. Seal edges together before cooking.

FRENCH TOAST WITH ORANGE SAUCE SUPREME

- **¼ cup frozen orange juice concentrate, thawed**
- **¼ cup water**
- **¼ cup butter or margarine**
- **½ cup sugar**
- **3 eggs**
- **3 tablespoons frozen orange juice concentrate, thawed**
- **¼ cup water**
- **¼ teaspoon salt**
- **12 slices French bread, cut 1-inch thick**

1. Combine ¼ cup concentrate, ¼ cup water, the butter and sugar in 2-cup glass measure.

2. Microwave for 2 to 2½ minutes, on HIGH, or until bubbly. Set aside.

3. Preheat microwave browning grill for 5 minutes on HIGH.

4. Combine eggs, 3 tablespoons concentrate, ¼ cup water and the salt in shallow bowl. Beat until smooth. Dip bread slices into mixture. Arrange 6 slices on preheated grill.

5. Microwave for 30 seconds on HIGH. Turn toast over and continue cooking for 1 to 1½ minutes, on HIGH, or until lightly browned and heated through.

6. Reheat microwave browning grill for 3½ minutes on HIGH. Cook remaining 6 slices of toast as directed.

7. Microwave toast and sauce for about 1 minute, on HIGH, or until serving temperature. About 4 Servings

FROZEN FRENCH TOAST

1. Preheat microwave browning grill for 5 minutes on HIGH.

2. Arrange 4 slices frozen French toast on preheated grill.

3. Microwave for 45 seconds on HIGH. Turn toast over and continue cooking for 45 to 60 seconds, on HIGH, or until heated. 4 Slices Toast

Make your own English muffins using frozen bread dough and your browning grill.

ENGLISH MUFFINS

1. Thaw one loaf frozen bread dough.

2. Divide dough into 12 equal balls. Sprinkle cornmeal over bottom of shallow baking pan. Place balls in pan and flatten to 3-inch circles. Turn circles over so both sides are coated with cornmeal.

3. Cover and let rise in warm place 1 to 1½ hours or until about 1 inch high.

4. Preheat microwave browning grill for 5 minutes on HIGH.

5. Arrange 6 muffins on preheated grill.

6. Microwave for 1 minute on HIGH. Turn muffins over and continue cooking for 2 to 2½ minutes, on HIGH, or until browned. Cool.

7. Reheat microwave browning grill for 2½ minutes on HIGH. Add muffins to grill and continue cooking muffins as directed. Split muffins apart with fork and toast just before serving.   12 Muffins

BUTTER-DIPPED BISCUITS

2 tablespoons butter or margarine
1 can (8 oz.) refrigerated biscuits
Sesame or poppy seed, if desired

1. Microwave butter in glass dish for 30 seconds, on HIGH, or until melted.

2. Preheat microwave browning grill for 5 minutes on HIGH.

3. Separate biscuit dough into 10 biscuits. Dip each in butter coating all sides; sprinkle with seeds. Arrange on preheated grill.

4. Microwave for 45 seconds on HIGH. Turn biscuits over and continue cooking for 45 to 60 seconds, on HIGH, or until no longer doughy.
                                                        10 Biscuits

GARLIC TOAST

¼ cup butter or margarine
¼ teaspoon garlic salt
8 slices French bread, cut ½-inch thick

1. Microwave butter and garlic salt in glass dish for about 30 seconds, on HIGH, or until melted.

2. Preheat microwave browning grill for 5 minutes on HIGH.

3. Brush each side of bread with butter mixture. Arrange slices, cut-side-down, on preheated grill.

4. Microwave for 1½ minutes on HIGH. Turn toast over and continue cooking for 1½ to 2 minutes, on HIGH, or until crisp. Serve warm or cold. 8 Slices Toast

eggs

If cooking eggs in the microwave makes you a bit uneasy, the microwave browning grill should do away with your fears. Gone is the danger of uneven cooking or even overcooking. Eggs are just a natural for the grill!

Of course, all eggs no matter how they are prepared, should be treated gently. And, preheating the browning grill for 5 minutes provides just the right amount of heat to help along the cooking process and offer delicate browning at the same time.

You will notice that the browning grill surface slopes gradually. This allows fats and juices to drain from meats as they cook. Naturally, you don't want your eggs sliding off the grill and a few simple techniques will keep them right where you want them.

For example, scrambled egg-type dishes are partially cooked before being placed on the grill. This helpful hint is described in detail in the chapter.

Unless the egg mixture you are using contains extra butter, greasing the grill surface or spraying it with a non-stick coating will save you clean-up time.

Pictured: Fried Egg, page 50.

For more than two eggs, individual foil "collars" hold eggs in place.

FRIED EGGS

1. Preheat microwave browning grill for 5 minutes on HIGH. Spray surface of preheated grill with non-stick vegetable coating or grease lightly.

2. Break eggs onto grill, holding in place with shell for a few seconds so they will not slip off grill.

3. Microwave on HIGH for:
      1 egg - 45 to 60 seconds
      2 eggs - 1 to 1½ minutes
      3 eggs* - 2 to 3 minutes
      4 eggs* - 2½ to 3½ minutes
      5 eggs* - 3 to 4 minutes

4. Let stand on grill a few minutes to finish cooking. Season with salt and pepper.

TIPS *With more than 2 eggs, make "collars" of foil to hold them in place on grill. Cut strips of foil 12 inches long and 2 inches wide. Fold the foil lengthwise 3 times to form a strip about ¾-inch wide. Bring ends of strip together and fold over several times to form a ring about 3 inches in diameter. Lightly grease rings and place on preheated grill. Break eggs one at a time into a cup. Carefully slip into ring while holding ring in place.

● When cooking more than 3 eggs and omitting the foil rings, the cooking time will be about 1 minute less.

● If you need to reheat the browning grill for additional eggs, microwave for 2½ minutes on HIGH.

Lightly grease grill to keep potato patties from sticking.

SPUDS 'N EGGS

    1 package (12 oz.) frozen hash browns
    ½ teaspoon salt
    1 tablespoon finely chopped onion
    2 tablespoons finely chopped green pepper
    5 eggs
    Salt and pepper

1. Microwave potatoes in package for 6 to 6½ minutes, on HIGH, or until thawed and partially cooked.

2. Preheat microwave browning grill for 5 minutes on HIGH.

3. Combine potatoes, salt, onion, green pepper and 1 egg.

4. Spray preheated grill with vegetable non-stick coating or grease lightly. Spoon mixture onto preheated grill forming 4 patties.

5. Microwave for 6 minutes on HIGH. Turn patties over and make an indentation in each large enough to hold an egg. Break an egg into each. Season with salt and pepper.

6. Microwave for 4½ to 5½ minutes, on HIGH, or until eggs are desired doneness. Season with salt and pepper. 4 Servings

TIP If you wish to use raw potatoes, shred about 3 cups. Precook in covered casserole as directed in step 1; continue with remaining directions.

EGGS 'N HASH

    1 can (15 oz.) corned beef hash
    2 tablespoons finely chopped green pepper
    4 eggs
    Salt and pepper

1. Preheat microwave browning grill for 5 minutes on HIGH.

2. Combine hash and green pepper. Spray surface of preheated grill with vegetable non-stick coating or grease lightly. Spoon hash mixture onto grill forming 4 patties. Make an indentation in each patty large enough to hold an egg. Break an egg into each. Sprinkle with salt and pepper.

3. Microwave for 7 to 8 minutes, on HIGH, or until eggs are desired doneness.   4 Servings

The egg mixture is partially cooked so it will hold its shape when on the grill.

EGGS FU YUNG

    Fu Yung Sauce (see below)
    6 eggs
    1 can (16 oz.) bean sprouts, drained
    ¼ cup chopped onion
    ¼ cup chopped green pepper
    2 tablespoons soy sauce
    2 tablespoons butter or margarine

1. Prepare Fu Yung Sauce.

2. Beat eggs in 1½-quart glass casserole. Mix in remaining ingredients. Cover with glass lid.

3. Microwave for 3 minutes on HIGH. Stir and continue cooking for 2½ to 3 minutes on HIGH. (Eggs will be only partially cooked).

4. Preheat microwave browning grill for 5 minutes on HIGH. Spray surface of preheated grill with vegetable non-stick coating or grease lightly. Spoon about half of egg mixture onto grill, forming 4 to 6 patties.

5. Microwave on HIGH for 1½ minutes. Turn patties over and continue cooking for 30 to 60 seconds, on HIGH, or until set.

6. Reheat microwave browning grill for 2½ minutes on HIGH. Spoon remaining egg mixture onto grill and continue cooking as directed. Serve with Fu Yung Sauce.   About 6 Servings

FU YUNG SAUCE

    2 tablespoons cornstarch
    2 teaspoons sugar
    2 tablespoons soy sauce
    2 tablespoons vinegar
    1 cup water

1. Combine all ingredients in 2-cup glass measure.

2. Microwave for 1½ minutes on HIGH. Stir mixture and continue cooking for 1 to 1½ minutes, on HIGH, or until mixture boils and thickens.
        About 1½ Cups Sauce

Undercook eggs slightly as they continue to cook after removal from oven.

ENGLISH BASKETS

2 English muffins, split
4 eggs
1 envelope hollandaise sauce mix

1. Preheat microwave browning grill for 5 minutes on HIGH.

2. Hollow out cut sides of muffins so each will hold an egg. Place cut-side-down on preheated grill.

3. Microwave for 1 minute, on HIGH, or until lightly toasted. Turn muffins over and break an egg into each hollow.

4. Microwave for 2½ to 3 minutes, on HIGH, or until eggs are desired doneness.

5. Prepare sauce mix in 2-cup glass measure adding ingredients as directed on package.

6. Microwave for 2 minutes on HIGH. Stir and continue cooking for 1 to 1½ minutes, on HIGH, or until mixture is thickened. Place baskets on serving plates. Spoon sauce over each.   4 Servings

Precooking the eggs helps keep them in position on the grill.

FARM-STYLE OMELET

5 eggs
⅓ cup milk
1 teaspoon salt
Dash pepper
2 tablespoons chopped onion
2 slices bacon
2 potatoes, cooked and cubed

1. Combine eggs, milk, salt and pepper in 1-quart glass casserole. Stir in onion. Cover with glass lid.

2. Microwave for 2 minutes on HIGH. Stir egg mixture and continue cooking for 1 minute on HIGH. (Eggs will be only partially cooked.) Set aside.

3. Preheat microwave browning grill for 5 minutes on HIGH. Place bacon slices on preheated grill.

4. Microwave for 4 to 4½ minutes, on HIGH, or until bacon is crisp. Remove bacon slices and set aside.

5. Reheat microwave browning grill for 2½ minutes on HIGH. Add crumbled bacon and potatoes to eggs. Carefully spoon onto preheated grill.

6. Microwave for 2 to 3 minutes, on HIGH, or until eggs are desired doneness. Fold over mixture while turning onto serving plate.   4 to 5 Servings

MEXICALI EGGS

>   5 **eggs**
> ⅓ **cup milk**
> ½ **teaspoon salt**
>   2 **tablespoons butter or margarine**
>   1 **cup shredded Monterey Jack cheese**
>   3 **tablespoons chopped green chilies**
>   1 **tomato, chopped**
>   4 **flour tortillas**

1. Beat together eggs, milk and salt in 1-quart glass casserole. Add butter. Cover with glass lid.

2. Microwave for 2 minutes on HIGH. Stir and continue cooking for 2 to 2½ minutes, on HIGH, or until eggs are almost set.

3. Preheat microwave browning grill for 5 minutes on HIGH.

4. Stir cheese, chilies and tomato into egg mixture. Place 2 tortillas on preheated grill.

5. Microwave for 1 minute on HIGH. Turn tortillas over and top with half of egg mixture. Continue cooking for 1 to 1½ minutes, on HIGH, or until heated.

6. Reheat microwave browning grill for 3½ minutes. Place remaining tortillas on grill and continue cooking as directed. 4 Servings

MINI CHILIES RELLANOS

>   1 **can (4 oz.) whole green chilies**
>   6 **sticks Monterey Jack, Cheddar**
> **or American cheese**
>   3 **eggs, separated**
> 1½ **tablespoons all-purpose flour**

1. Rinse chilies being careful to remove all seeds. Cut each chilie in half crosswise. Stuff each with cheese stick; set aside.

2. Preheat microwave browning grill for 5 minutes on HIGH.

3. Beat egg whites in small mixing bowl until stiff peaks form. Beat yolks with flour in small bowl; fold yolk mixture into egg whites.

4. Spray surface of preheated grill with non-stick vegetable coating or grease lightly. Spoon about ½ cup of egg mixture onto grill forming 3 omelets at a time; gently spread out. Place a stuffed chilie on one end of each omelet.

5. Microwave for 30 seconds on HIGH. Fold the one end of each omelet over the end with chilie. Continue cooking for 30 to 60 seconds, on HIGH, or until egg is set.

6. Reheat microwave browning grill for 2 minutes on HIGH. Continue cooking remaining egg mixture as directed. 6 Rellanos

TIP These are quite spicy. If you prefer a milder flavor, reduce the amount of green chilies or substitute some pimento.

vegetables

Old-fashioned vegetables in a new fashioned way —
with a little streamlined assistance from the microwave
browning grill.

Before these garden fresh favorites are sautéed to a
nutritious, golden goodness, they can be dressed for
company in a crisp coating of buttery crumbs. Or,
laced with a simple, well-seasoned sauce. Plain or
fancy, all the monotony of eating them just because
"they are good for you" will be gone.

Although some slow-to-cook vegetables will require
partial cooking with just microwaves before final browning on the grill, other jiffy-cook types grill easily to the
desired tender-crisp stage with no precooking.

You will notice a suggested 5-minute preheat time for
most of the vegetable recipes in this chapter. How
come? Well, this few minutes of "warm up" time provides the grill with enough heat to tenderly brown without any danger of overcooking even the most temper-
mental vegetables.

*Pictured: Sautéed Cabbage Wedges, page 61; Grilled
Tomatoes, page 60.*

Thinly sliced potatoes cook on the grill without precooking.

SAUTEED POTATO SLICES

⅔ **cup butter or margarine, melted**
4 **medium potatoes, peeled**
1½ **teaspoons onion salt**
1 **teaspoon dried parsley flakes**

1. Microwave butter in glass dish for 1 to 1½ minutes, on HIGH, or until melted.

2. Preheat microwave browning grill for 5 minutes on HIGH.

3. Slice potatoes crosswise into ¼-inch slices. Add onion salt and parsley to butter. Dip slices into butter.

4. Arrange a layer of slices on preheated grill.

5. Microwave for 5 minutes on HIGH. Turn potatoes over and continue cooking for 5 to 6 minutes, on HIGH, or until tender.

6. Reheat microwave browning grill for 2½ minutes on HIGH. Place remaining potatoes on grill and cook as directed.   4 to 6 Servings

The browning grill gives these frozen potatoes a crunchy crust.

SPEEDY POTATO PUFFS

1. Preheat microwave browning grill for 5 minutes on HIGH.

2. Coat preheated grill with 1 tablespoon butter or margarine. Place 1 package (16 oz.) frozen potato puff logs on grill.

3. Microwave for 3 minutes on HIGH. Turn potatoes over and continue cooking for 3 to 4 minutes, on HIGH, or until lightly browned. 4 to 5 Servings

Start with cold potatoes for easier shaping.

CRUNCHY-COATED POTATO PATTIES

2 **cups cold mashed potatoes**
1 **egg, slightly beaten**
2 **teaspoons chopped chives**
⅔ **cup crushed cheese crackers**

1. Combine potatoes, egg and chives. Sprinkle crackers on wax paper.

2. Preheat microwave browning grill for 5 minutes on HIGH.

3. Drop heaping tablespoonfuls of potato mixture onto cracker crumbs, forming into patties and coating with crumbs.

4. Spray surface of preheated grill with vegetable non-stick coating or grease lightly. Place patties on grill.

5. Microwave for 2 minutes on HIGH. Turn patties over and continue cooking for 2 to 2½ minutes, on HIGH, or until heated through.   4 to 6 Servings

TIP Instant potatoes can be used for mashed potatoes. Just add ¼ cup extra potatoes to the directions for 4 servings. Chill thoroughly before preparing patties. The liquid for the potatoes will require about 4 minutes to boil in the microwave.

SMOKY POTATO STICKS

> **4 large potatoes, peeled**
> **¼ cup water**
> **¼ cup cooking oil**
> **½ teaspoon liquid smoke**
> **1 cup grated Parmesan cheese**
> **1½ teaspoons seasoned salt**

1. Cut potatoes lengthwise into sticks about ½-inch thick. Place in 2-quart glass casserole. Combine water, cooking oil and liquid smoke; add to potatoes. Cover with glass lid.

2. Microwave for 8 to 9 minutes, on HIGH, or until potatoes are partially cooked. Drain; set aside.

3. Preheat microwave browning grill for 5 minutes on HIGH.

4. Combine cheese and salt. Coat partially cooked potato sticks with mixture.

5. Spray preheated grill with vegetable non-stick coating or grease lightly. Arrange a layer of potatoes on grill.

6. Microwave for 2 minutes on HIGH. Turn potatoes over and continue cooking for 3 to 4 minutes, on HIGH, or until tender.

7. Reheat microwave browning grill for 4 minutes on HIGH. Place remaining potatoes on grill and continue cooking as directed.   4 to 6 Servings

Flattening patties shortens cooking time.

HOME-STYLE POTATO PATTIES

> **4 medium potatoes, peeled**
> **1 cup shredded Cheddar cheese**
> **1 egg**
> **2 tablespoons chopped green onion**
> **1 teaspoon salt**
> **⅛ teaspoon pepper**

1. Coarsely shred potatoes into large mixing bowl.

2. Preheat microwave browning grill for 5 minutes on HIGH.

3. Add cheese, egg, onion, salt and pepper to potatoes; mix well.

4. Coat surface of preheated grill with vegetable non-stick coating or grease lightly. Spoon about half of potato mixture onto grill forming 4 patties. Flatten each patty.

5. Microwave for 4 minutes on HIGH. Turn patties over and continue cooking for 2 to 3 minutes, on HIGH, or until potatoes are tender.

6. Reheat microwave browning grill for 3½ minutes on HIGH. Spoon remaining potatoes onto grill and continue as directed.   6 to 8 Servings

TIP If desired, substitute 4 cups frozen shredded hash browns for shredded potatoes. Microwave potatoes for 4 minutes on HIGH to thaw before adding remaining ingredients.

Precook these frozen potatoes to assure tenderness.

QUICK HASH BROWNS

1. Microwave 1 package (12 oz.) frozen shredded hash browns in package for 5 to 6 minutes, on HIGH, or until thawed.

2. Preheat microwave browning grill for 5 minutes on HIGH.

3. Spread about 1 teaspoon softened butter or margarine on each hash brown patty. Place buttered-side-down on preheated grill.

4. Microwave for 4 minutes on HIGH. Turn patties over and continue cooking for 3 to 4 minutes, on HIGH, or until tender.   About 4 Servings

SNO-CAPPED SWEETS

    1 can (18 oz.) sweet potatoes, drained
    ¼ cup packed brown sugar
    2 tablespoons butter or margarine
    6 large marshmallows

1. Preheat microwave browning grill for 5 minutes on HIGH.

2. Mash sweet potatoes. Spoon potatoes onto preheated grill forming 6 mounds. Make a depression in the center of each mound.

3. Microwave for 1 minute on HIGH. Divide brown sugar and butter among mounds. Top each with a marshmallow.

4. Microwave for 1½ to 2 minutes, on HIGH, or until marshmallows are puffed.   6 Servings

REFRIED BEANS

    3 slices bacon
    1 can (15 oz.) pinto beans, drained
    ¼ teaspoon salt
    1 tablespoon chopped pimento
    ¼ cup shredded Cheddar or Monterey Jack cheese

1. Preheat microwave browning grill for 4 minutes on HIGH. Lay strips of bacon on grill.

2. Microwave for 3 minutes on HIGH. Turn bacon over and continue cooking for 1 to 1½ minutes, on HIGH, or until bacon is crisp. Set aside bacon; reserve bacon drippings.

3. Reheat microwave browning grill for 3 minutes on HIGH.

4. Mash beans in large bowl. Add bacon fat and salt; mix until blended. Stir in pimento and crumbled bacon.

5. Spoon beans onto preheated grill, keeping them atop grill surface.

6. Microwave for 2 mintues on HIGH. Stir or turn beans over and continue cooking for 1 to 2 minutes, on HIGH, or until heated. Spoon into serving dish; sprinkle with cheese.   3 to 4 Servings

SAUTEED ACORN RINGS WITH MAPLE GLAZE

1 acorn squash
3 tablespoons butter or margarine, softened
⅓ cup maple-flavored syrup
¼ teaspoon salt

1. Microwave whole squash for 4 minutes on HIGH. Turn squash over and continue cooking for 3 to 4 mintues, on HIGH, or until hot and slightly soft to the touch.

2. Preheat microwave browing grill for 5 minutes on HIGH.

3. Cut squash crosswise into 1-inch slices. Remove seeds. Spread one side of slices with 1 tablespoon of the butter.

4. Place squash rings buttered-side-down on preheated grill.

5. Microwave for 3 minutes on HIGH. Turn rings over and continue cooking for 3 to 4 minutes, on HIGH, or until squash is tender. Let stand on grill.

6. Microwave remaining butter in glass dish for 30 to 45 seconds, on HIGH, or until bubbly. Stir in syrup and salt. Place squash rings on serving platter. Spoon syrup mixture over squash.   3 to 4 Servings

SAVORY-FILLED SQUASH HALVES

1 acorn squash
1 small onion, sliced
3 tablespoons butter or margarine
Salt
1 teaspoon dried parsley flakes

1. Microwave whole squash for 4 minutes on HIGH. Turn squash over and continue cooking for 3 to 4 minutes, on HIGH, or until slightly soft to the touch. Let stand a few minutes.

2. Combine onion and 2 tablespoons of the butter in small glass dish.

3. Microwave for 2 minutes on HIGH. Stir and continue cooking for 2 to 3 minutes, on HIGH, or until tender.

4. Preheat microwave browning grill for 5 minutes on HIGH. Cut squash in half crosswise; scoop out seeds. Spread remaining tablespoon of butter on cut edges of squash.

5. Place squash halves cut-side-down on preheated grill.

6. Microwave for 3 minutes on HIGH. Turn squash cut-side-up (if necessary, cut off pointed end so squash will not tip). Season with salt. Spoon onion slices into squash halves. Sprinkle with parsley.

7. Microwave for 3 to 4 minutes, on HIGH, or until heated and tender.
                    2 Servings

Select firm tomatoes and avoid overcooking.

COTTAGE TOMATO SLICES

> 1 **tablespoon butter or margarine**
> 3 **medium tomatoes, cut into ½-inch slices**
> ½ **cup crushed cheese crackers**
> ¾ **cup creamed cottage cheese**
> ⅛ **teaspoon salt**
> ⅛ **teaspoon leaf basil**

1. Microwave butter in glass dish for 30 to 45 seconds, on HIGH, or until melted.

2. Preheat microwave browning grill for 5 minutes on HIGH.

3. Slice tomatoes; dip each slice into melted butter. Coat with cracker crumbs. Combine cottage cheese, salt and basil.

4. Place tomato slices on preheated grill. Spoon cottage cheese mixture onto each; sprinkle with any remaining crumbs.

5. Microwave for 2 to 2½ minutes, on HIGH, or until cheese just starts to bubble. 4 to 5 Servings

TIP Tomatoes are also good just coated with crumbs and browned on each side.

Dipping tomatoes in butter helps the crumbs adhere evenly.

GRILLED TOMATOES

> 2 **tablespoons butter or margarine**
> 3 **medium tomatoes**
> ½ **cup crushed salad croutons**

1. Microwave butter in glass dish for 30 to 45 seconds, on HIGH, or until melted.

2. Preheat microwave browning grill for 5 minutes on HIGH. Cut each tomato into 3 slices; trim end slices so they will lie flat on grill.

3. Dip tomato in melted butter; coat with crushed croutons. Place on pre-heated grill.

4. Microwave for 1 minute on HIGH. Turn slices over and continue cooking for 1 to 1½ minutes, on HIGH, or until tomatoes are heated.

About 6 Servings

GOLDEN MUSHROOMS

> ½ **cup butter or margarine**
> 1 **teaspoon garlic salt**
> 2 **cups (8 oz.) fresh mushrooms**

1. Microwave butter in medium glass dish for 45 to 60 seconds, on HIGH, or until melted. Stir in garlic salt.

2. Preheat microwave browning grill for 5 minutes on HIGH.

3. Wash mushrooms; halve or slice each lengthwise. Stir into butter mixture, coating with butter.

4. Place mushrooms on preheated grill.

5. Microwave for 1 minute on HIGH. Turn mushrooms over and continue cooking for 1 to 2 minutes, on HIGH, or until tender. About 4 Servings

EGGPLANT ITALIANO

1 large eggplant, peeled
2 eggs, beaten
1¼ cups dry bread crumbs
1 can (15 oz.) tomato sauce
½ teaspoon Worcestershire sauce
1 teaspoon leaf oregano
2 cups (8 oz.) shredded Mozzarella cheese

1. Preheat microwave browning grill for 5 minutes on HIGH.

2. Slice eggplant into ½-inch slices. Dip each slice into beaten egg; coat with crumbs.

3. Place about half of slices on preheated grill.

4. Microwave for 3 minutes on HIGH. Turn slices over and continue cooking for 2 to 3 minutes, on HIGH, or until just about tender. Place slices in 2½-quart glass casserole.

5. Reheat microwave browning grill for 2½ minutes on HIGH. Add remaining slices to grill and cook as directed.

6. Combine tomato sauce, Worcestershire sauce and oregano. Spoon half of mixture over eggplant in casserole. Top with half of cheese. Add remaining eggplant slices, sauce and cheese. Cover with glass lid.

7. Microwave for 5 to 6 minutes, on HIGH, or until bubbly throughout.

5 to 6 Servings

Microwaving cabbage minimizes "after odor."

SAUTEED CABBAGE WEDGES

¼ cup butter or margarine
½ head cabbage
2 tablespoons grated Parmesan cheese
Salt and pepper

1. Microwave butter in glass dish for 45 to 60 seconds, on HIGH, or until melted.

2. Preheat microwave browning grill for 5 minutes on HIGH.

3. Cut cabbage into 6 to 8 wedges. Dip each into butter. Sprinkle with cheese.

4. Place slices on preheated grill.

5. Microwave for 2 minutes on HIGH. Turn slices over and continue cooking for 2½ to 3 minutes, on HIGH, or until desired doneness. Season to taste.

6 to 8 Servings

TIPS The Parmesan cheese can be omitted if desired.

● Butter and cheese can be omitted and cabbage wedges spread with ¼ cup Thousand Island salad dressing before browning on grill.

desserts

Did someone say "What's for dessert?" Whether it's freshly baked cookies, a simple fruit finale or a more substantial cake treat, desserts are the something extra that make a conventional menu special.

You will find the microwave browning grill to be helpful, especially for fruit and cake desserts where a little additional browning and toasty flavor are desired. Frozen cakes are thawed beautifully by the time the edges become golden. Other sweet favorites, which normally require sautéing, adapt handsomely to browning on the versatile grill.

And just imagine — for making a few candy-type cookies, the grill is transformed into a baking pan. Since the surface absorbs heat and continues to heat throughout the cooking process, the bottoms of the cookies become golden brown while the rest cook evenly and easily.

No doubt, you will use your browning grill less for desserts than for other courses, but after trying these recipe ideas, you will be happy to have it handy for hurry-up goodies for the sweet tooth.

Pictured: Toasted Pound Cake with Lemon Sauce, page 65.

Stir cream slowly into butter mixture to avoid curdling.

BUTTER SAUCE FOR GRILLED FRUITS

    ¼ **cup butter or margarine**
    ½ **cup packed brown sugar**
    ½ **cup light cream**
    2 **tablespoons brandy or 2 teaspoons brandy extract**

1. Combine butter and brown sugar in 4-cup glass measure.

2. Microwave for 30 to 60 seconds, on HIGH, or until butter is melted. Slowly stir in cream.

3. Microwave for 1 to 1½ minutes, on HIGH, or until mixture just starts to bubble. Stir in brandy. Serve over Grilled Pineapple or Bananas.

                                           About 1 Cup Sauce

GRILLED FRESH PINEAPPLE

1. Peel 1 fresh pineapple. Cut into slices ½-inch thick; remove core from each.

2. Preheat microwave browning grill for 5 minutes on HIGH.

3. Place pineapple slices on grill. Dot each slice with a scant teaspoon of butter or margarine.

4. Microwave for 4 minutes on HIGH. Turn slices over and continue cooking for 1 to 1½ minutes, on HIGH, or until heated.

5. Reheat microwave browning grill for 3 minutes on HIGH. Place remaining slices on grill and cook as directed. Serve warm with Butter Sauce (above).

                                              4 to 6 Servings

Select firm, slightly under ripe bananas.

GRILLED BANANAS

1. Preheat microwave browning grill for 5 minutes on HIGH.

2. Peel 3 bananas. Slice each once in half crosswise and then in half lengthwise. Spread about 1 tablespoon softened butter or margarine over cut sides.

3. Place bananas cut-side-down on preheated grill.

4. Microwave for 1 to 1¼ minutes, on HIGH, or until warmed and lightly browned. Serve warm with Butter Sauce (above). If desired, garnish with a few chopped nuts or toasted almonds.   4 to 6 Servings

FRUIT-FILLED CAKES

    4 individual shortcake bases
    1 cup (half a 21-oz. can) prepared fruit pie filling
    Whipped cream or ice cream

1. Preheat microwave browning grill for 2½ minutes on HIGH. Place 4 short-cakes top-side-down on grill.

2. Microwave for 1 minute on HIGH. Turn shortcakes over; spoon about ¼ cup fruit filling into each. Continue cooking for 1½ to 2 minutes, on HIGH, or until base is lightly toasted and filling is heated. Serve warm topped with whipped cream or ice cream.   4 Servings

TIP If preparing more than 4 shortcakes, reheat grill 1½ minutes. Cook shortcakes as directed.

Toast cake just until warm to avoid overcooking.

TOASTED POUND CAKE WITH LEMON SAUCE

    ½ cup sugar
    2 tablespoons cornstarch
    ¼ teaspoon salt
    1 cup water
    2 teaspoons grated lemon peel
    ¼ cup lemon juice
    1 tablespoon butter or margarine
    1 frozen pound cake (10¾ oz.)
    2 tablespoons butter or margarine, softened

1. Combine sugar, cornstarch and salt in 4-cup glass measure. Stir in water.

2. Microwave for 2 minutes on HIGH. Stir mixture and continue cooking for 1 to 2 minutes, on HIGH, or until mixture boils. Stir in lemon peel and juice and 1 tablespoon butter.

3. Preheat microwave browning grill for 4 minutes on HIGH.

4. Remove frozen cake from pan. Cut cake into 8 slices. Spread one side of each slice with softened butter.

5. Place slices buttered-side-down on preheated grill.

6. Microwave for 1 minute on HIGH. Turn slices over and continue cooking for 30 to 60 seconds, on HIGH, or until heated. Serve with warm Lemon Sauce.   About 8 Servings

See simple envelope-style folding instructions below.

BLINTZES

> **About 16 crêpes**
> **1 cup dry curd cottage cheese**
> **½ cup sour cream**
> **1 egg**
> **2 tablespoons sugar**
> **½ tablespoon lemon juice**
> **2 tablespoons butter or margarine, softened**

1. Prepare crêpes, see next page.

2. Combine cheese, sour cream, egg, sugar and lemon juice. Place crêpes with most attractive side down. Spoon about 1 tablespoon of cheese mixture onto center of each crêpe. Fold two sides over to meet in center. Then, fold other two sides in so they overlap and enclose filling. Place folded-side-down on tray or plate.

3. Preheat microwave browning grill for 4½ minutes on HIGH. Spread top side of each blintz with butter. Arrange half of blintzes buttered-side-down on preheated grill.

4. Microwave for 1 minute on HIGH. Turn blintzes over and continue cooking for 1½ to 2 minutes, on HIGH, or until heated through.

5. Reheat microwave browning grill for 3 minutes on HIGH. Continue cooking remaining blintzes as directed. Serve warm with sweetened fresh fruits or prepared fruit pie filling.   About 16 Blintzes

TIPS The crêpes can be filled early in the day and then refrigerated. Just heat on the browning grill at serving time. Or, they can be totally prepared ahead and reheated on a glass serving plate at serving time.

● The Orange Sauce Supreme with the French Toast recipe, page 46, is also good served with the Blintzes.

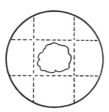 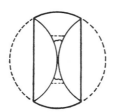 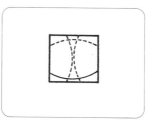

Filling in center.   *First fold.*   *Second fold.*

Dip-style crêpe pans require a thicker batter.

CREPES

 4 eggs
 1 cup milk
 ¼ cup water
 1 cup unsifted all-purpose flour
 1 tablespoon sugar
 ½ teaspoon salt
 2 tablespoons cooking oil

1. Combine all ingredients. Beat with rotary beater just until smooth. Allow to stand in refrigerator a few minutes for bubbles to break.

2. Heat crêpe pan or 9-inch frying pan over medium high heat. Grease pan lightly. Pour a scant ¼ cup (about 3 tablespoons) batter into pan, quickly tilting pan so batter covers bottom evenly. Cook until edges just begin to brown and top is nearly dry. Turn over and cook other side. Invert pan over plate so crêpe falls out of pan. Continue cooking crêpes, stacking one atop another with most attractive side down. If not using immediately, cover with plastic wrap to prevent drying.   About 16 Crêpes

TIP When using a dip-style crêpe pan, decrease milk to ⅔ cup. Heat the pan, dip it into the batter and cook as directed. Since these crêpes will be a little thinner, you will probably have more than the 16, but you can just use a little less filling in each one.

A baking apple keeps it shape better than the eating variety.

RING AROUND APPLES

 ¼ cup butter or margarine
 ¼ cup sugar
 2 teaspoons cinnamon
 2 apples

1. Microwave butter in glass dish for 30 to 45 seconds, on HIGH, or until melted. Mix in sugar and cinnamon.

2. Preheat microwave browning grill for 4 minutes on HIGH.

3. Core apples; cut crosswise into ¼-inch thick slices. Coat each slice with butter mixture. Place on preheated grill.

4. Microwave for 1 minute on HIGH. Turn slices over and continue cooking for 1½ to 2 minutes, on HIGH, or until apples are tender.   3 to 4 Servings

ANGEL SUNDAES

> **Chocolate Fudge Sauce (see below)**
> **6 slices angel food cake, cut ¾-inch thick**
> **1 tablespoon butter or margarine**
> **Ice cream**

1. Prepare Sauce; set aside.

2. Preheat microwave browning grill for 4 minutes on HIGH.

3. Butter one side of each cake slice. Place buttered-side-down on preheated grill.

4. Microwave for 1 to 1½ minutes, on HIGH, or until lightly browned. Place in serving dishes with toasted side up. Top with scoop of ice cream and plenty of Chocolate Fudge Sauce. 6 Servings

TIP Three cake doughnuts can be substituted for cake slices. Split doughnuts and toast cut sides on grill as directed.

The kind of sauce that turns to fudge on ice cream.

CHOCOLATE FUDGE SAUCE

> **1 square (1 oz.) unsweetened chocolate**
> **¼ cup butter or margarine**
> **⅓ cup light cream**
> **½ cup powdered sugar**
> **6 large marshmallows**
> **1 teaspoon vanilla**

1. Combine chocolate and butter in 4-cup glass measure.

2. Microwave for 1 to 1½ minutes, on HIGH, or until chocolate is melted.

3. Stir in cream and powdered sugar; beat until smooth. Add marshmallows.

4. Microwave for 45 to 60 seconds, on HIGH, or until marshmallows are puffed. Add vanilla; beat until smooth. 1¼ Cups Sauce

If the cookies start to brown too much on the bottom, allow the grill to cool about 5 minutes.

QUICK MACAROONS

> **5 cups (about 14 ozs.) flaked coconut**
> **1 can (14 oz.) sweetened condensed milk**
> **1 teaspoon vanilla**
> **½ cup chopped nuts**

1. Combine all ingredients; mix well.

2. Preheat microwave browning grill for 1 minute on HIGH. Spray surface of preheated grill with vegetable non-stick coating or grease lightly. Drop macaroons by teaspoonfuls onto preheated grill.

3. Microwave for 3½ to 4 minutes, on HIGH, or until tops are just about set. Let stand 1 minute. Remove from grill.

4. Do not reheat grill; just spoon more macaroon mixture onto grill and continue cooking as directed. About 48 Macaroons

TIP After spooning macaroon mixture onto grill, each macaroon can be topped with a chocolate piece or nut.

index

a

About Microwave Grill Browning 3-4
Acorn Rings with Maple Glaze,
 Sautéed 59
Angel Sundaes 68
Appetizers 16-23
 Appetizer Meatballs 18
 Cheese Melts 22
 Cheese 'n Bacon Toasties 21
 Cheesy Tortilla Turnovers 19
 Croque Monsieur 19
 Frozen Pizza Rolls 23
 Meatball Sauce 18
 Micro Wontons 23
 Mini Pizzas 23
 Parmesan Nibblers 20
 Sweet 'n Sour Kabobs 18
 Tomato Topper Canapés 21
 Tuna Toastwiches 20
Apples, Ring Around 67

b

Bacon, Canadian 34
Bacon, Egg and Toast Breakfast 10
Bacon Toasties, Cheese 'n 21
Bananas, Grilled 64
Barbecued Chops, Zippy 30
Bean Cakes, Mexican 37
Beans, Refried 58
Beef
 Appetizer Meatballs 18
 Filets Mignons with
  Butter-Mustard Sauce 28
 Glorified Hamburger Patties 26
 Grilled Family Steak 29
 Hamburger and Fries Lunch 13
 Liver, Bacon and Onions 35
 "Mock" Filets 28
 Open-Faced Hamburgers 44
 Parmesan Beef Patties 26
 Sirloin au Poivre 29
 Steak and Hash Browns Dinner 14
 Sweet-Sour Meatballs 27
 Swiss Minute Steaks 26
 Teriyaki Steak 27

Biscuits, Refrigerated
 Butter-Dipped Biscuits 47
 Wieners in Blankets 43
Blintzes 66
Bologna Burgers 43
Bratwurst 34
Breaded Fish Portions 39
Breaded Smoked Chops 30
Breads 45-47
 Butter-Dipped Biscuits 47
 English Muffins 47
 French Toast with Orange Sauce
  Supreme 46
 Frozen French Toast 46
 Garlic Toast 47
 Sour Cream Scones 45
Browning, How it Happens 3
Brunch Muffins 45
Butter-Dipped Biscuits 47
Butter Sauce for Grilled Fruits 64

c

Cabbage Wedges, Sautéed 61
Cakes
 Angel Sundaes 68
 Fruit-Filled Cakes 65
 Toasted Pound Cake with
  Lemon Sauce 65
Canadian Bacon 34
Casseroles, see Main Dishes
Cheese
 Bologna Burgers 43
 Cheese Melts 22
 Cheese 'n Bacon Toasties 21
 Cheesy Tortilla Turnovers 19
 Croque Monsieur 19
 Grilled Cheese Sandwiches 42
 Mexicali Eggs 53
 Mini Chilies Rellanos 53
 Open-Faced Cheese 'n Tomato
  Sandwiches 42
 Parmesan Nibblers 20
 Tuna Toastwiches 20
Cheesy Caesar Fish Fillets 38
Chicken
 Chicken Breast with Rice Dinner .. 15
 Chicken Cordon Bleu 36
 Crusty Fried Chicken 36
Chilies Rellanos, Mini 53
Chocolate Fudge Sauce 68
Cleaning Grill 4
Cookies, see Quick Macaroons 68
Cooking Chart 7
Corned Beef
 Eggs 'n Hash 51
 Grilled Reubens 42
Cottage Tomato Slices 60
Crêpes 67
Croque Monsieur 19
Croquettes, Tuna and Macaroni 37
Crunchy-Coated Potato Patties 56
Crusty Fried Chicken 36

d

Desserts 62-68
  Angel Sundaes 68
  Blintzes 66
  Butter Sauce for Grilled Fruits 64
  Chocolate Fudge Sauce 68
  Crepes 67
  Fruit-Filled Cakes 65
  Grilled Bananas 64
  Grilled Fresh Pineapple 64
  Quick Macaroons 68
  Ring Around Apples 67
  Toasted Pound Cake with
    Lemon Sauce 65

e

Egg Rolls, see Micro Wontons 23
Eggplant Italiano 61
Eggs 48-53
  Bacon-Egg and Toast Breakfast 10
  Brunch Muffins 45
  Eggs Fu Yung 51
  Eggs 'n Hash 51
  English Baskets 52
  Farm-Style Omelet 52
  Fried Eggs 50
  Mexicali Eggs 53
  Mini Chilies Rellanos 53
  Spuds 'n Eggs 50
English Muffins 47
  Brunch Muffins 45
  English Baskets 52

f

Family Steak, Grilled 29
Farm-Style Omelet 52
Filets Mignons with
  Butter-Mustard Sauce 28
Filets, "Mock" 28
Fillet of Sole Rolls 38
Fish
  Breaded Fish Portions 39
  Cheesy Caesar Fish Fillets 38
  Fillet of Sole Rolls 38
  Fish Sticks 39
  Sesame Salmon Steaks 39
  Tuna and Macaroni Croquettes 37
  Tuna Toastwiches 20
Flank Steak
  "Mock" Filets 28
  Teriyaki Steak 27
French Fries, see Hamburger
  and Fries Lunch 13
French Toast with Orange Sauce
  Supreme 46
Fried Eggs 50

Frozen
  Breaded Fish Portions 39
  Fish Sticks 39
  French Toast 46
  Pizza 44
  Pizza Rolls 23
  Quick Hash Browns 58
  Speedy Potato Puffs 56
Fruit-Filled Cakes 65
Fruits
  Grilled Bananas 64
  Grilled Fresh Pineapple 64
  Ring Around Apples 67
Fu Yung, Eggs 51
Fu Yung Sauce 51

g

Garlic Toast 47
Glorified Hamburger Patties 26
Golden Mushroom 60
Grilled Bananas 64
Grilled Cheese Sandwiches 42
Grilled Family Steak 29
Grilled Fresh Pineapple 64
Grilled Fruits, Butter Sauce for 64
Grilled Knackwurst 35
Grilled Lamb Chops 33
Grilled Reubens 42
Grilled Tomatoes 60
Ground Beef
  Glorified Hamburger Patties 26
  Hamburger and Fries Lunch 13
  Open-Faced Hamburgers 44
  Parmesan Beef Patties 26
  Sweet-Sour Meatballs 27

h

Ham
  Chicken Cordon Bleu 36
  Croque Monsieur 19
  Ham Slices with Orange Sauce 31
  Mexican Bean Cakes 37
Hamburger and Fries Lunch 13
Hamburger Patties, Glorified 26
Hamburgers, Open-Faced 44
Hash Browns
  Home-Style Potato Patties 57
  Quick Hash Browns 58
  Spuds 'n Eggs 50
Hints for Using Grill 5

k

Kabobs, Lamb 33
Kabobs, Sweet 'n Sour 18
Knackwurst, Grilled 35

l

Lamb
  Grilled Lamb Chops 33
  Lamb Kabobs 33
  Orange-Sparked Lamb Patties 32
Liver, Bacon and Onions 35

m

Macaroni Croquettes, Tuna and 37
Macaroons, Quick 68
Main Courses 24-39
Main Dishes
  Eggplant Italiano 61
  Mexican Bean Cakes 37
  Tuna and Macaroni Croquettes 37
  Veal Parmigiana 32
Meals 8-15
  Bacon, Egg and Toast Breakfast 10
  Chicken Breast with Rice Dinner ... 15
  Hamburger and Fries Lunch 13
  Pancakes and Sausage Breakfast ... 11
  Pork Chop and Hash Browns Dinner . 14
  Sandwich and Apple Lunch 12
  Steak and Hash Browns Dinner 14
Meatball Sauce 18
Meatballs, Appetizer 18
Meatballs, Sweet-Sour 27
Meats 24-35
  (see also Beef, Pork, etc.)
Mexican
  Cheesy Tortilla Turnovers 19
  Mexicali Eggs 53
  Mexican Bean Cakes 37
  Mini Chilies Rellanos 53
  Refried Beans 58
Micro Wontons 23
Mini Pizzas 22
Minute Steak, Swiss 26
"Mock" Filets 28
Mushrooms, Golden 60

o

Omelet, Farm-Style 52
Open-Faced Cheese 'n Tomato
  Sandwiches 42
Open-Faced Hamburgers 44
Orange-Sparked Lamb Patties 32
Oriental
  Eggs Fu Yung 51
  Fu Yung Sauce 51
  Micro Wontons 23

p

Pancakes, see Time Chart 7
Pancakes and Sausage Breakfast 11
Parmesan Beef Patties 26
Parmesan Nibblers 20
Parmigiana, Veal 32
Pineapple, Grilled Fresh 64
Pizza
  Deluxe Frozen Pizza 44
  Frozen Pizza 44
  Frozen Pizza Rolls 23
  Mini Pizzas 22
Pork
  Bratwurst 34
  Breaded Smoked Chops 30
  Canadian Bacon 34
  Ham Slices with Orange Sauce 31
  Knackwurst 35
  Pork Chop and Hash Browns Dinner . 14
  Sausage Links 34
  Sausage Patties 34
  Wiener Schnitzel 31
  Zippy Barbecued Chops 30
Potatoes
  Crunchy-Coated Potato Patties 56
  Farm-Style Omelet 52
  Home-Style Potato Patties 57
  Quick Hash Browns 58
  Sautéed Potato Slices 56
  Smoky Potato Sticks 57
  Speedy Potato Puffs 56
  Spuds 'n Eggs 50
Poultry
  Chicken Breast with Rice Dinner ... 15
  Chicken Cordon Bleu 36
  Crusty Fried Chicken 36
Pound Cake with Lemon Sauce,
  Toasted 65
Preheating Times 4

q

Quick Hash Browns 58
Quick Macaroons 68

r

Refried Beans 58
Rellanos, Mini Chilies 53
Reubens, Grilled 42
Ring Around Apples 67

s

Salmon Steaks, Sesame 39
Sandwich and Apple Lunch 12
Sandwiches 40-45
  Bologna Burgers 43
  Brunch Muffins 45
  Croque Monsieur 19
  Deluxe Frozen Pizza 44
  Frozen Pizza 44
  Grilled Cheese Sandwiches 42
  Grilled Reubens 42
  Open-Faced Cheese 'n Tomato
    Sandwiches..................... 42
  Open-Faced Hamburgers 44
  Wieners in Blankets 43
Sauces
  Butter-Mustard Sauce 28
  Butter Sauce for Grilled Fruits 64
  Chocolate Fudge Sauce 68
  Fu Yung Sauce 51
  Lemon Sauce 65
  Meatball Sauce 18
  Mushroom Sauce................. 29
  Orange Sauce 31
  Orange Sauce Supreme 46
Sausages
  Bratwurst 34
  Knackwurst 35
  Links 34
  Patties 34
  Sweet 'n Sour Kabobs 18
  Wieners 34
Sautéed Cabbage Wedges 61
Sautéed Potato Slices 56
Savory-Filled Squash Halves 59
Scones, Sour Cream............... 45
Sesame Salmon Steaks 39
Sirloin au Poivre 29
Smoked Pork Chops, Breaded 30
Smoky Potato Sticks 57
Snacks, see Appetizers
Sno-Capped Sweets 58
Sole Rolls, Fillet of 38
Sour Cream Scones 45
Speedy Potato Puffs 56
Spuds 'n Eggs 50
Squash
  Sautéed Acorn Rings with
    Maple Glaze 59
  Savory-Filled Squash Halves 59
  Zucchini, see Chicken Breast
    Dinner......................... 15
Steaks
  Filets Mignons with
    Butter-Mustard Sauce 28
  Grilled Family Steak 29
  "Mock" Filets 28
  Sirloin au Poivre 29
  Steak and Hash Browns Dinner 14
  Swiss Minute Steaks 26
  T-Bones with Mushroom Sauce 29
  Teriyaki Steak 27
Steps to Microwave Browning 6
Sweet 'n Sour Kabobs 18
Sweet-Sour Meatballs 27
Sweets, Sno-Capped 58
Swiss Minute Steaks 26

t

T-Bones with Mushroom Sauce 29
Teriyaki Steak 27
Time Chart 7
Toast, Garlic 47
Toasted Pound Cake with
  Lemon Sauce 65
Tomatoes
  Cottage Tomato Slices 60
  Grilled Tomatoes 60
  Open-Faced Cheese 'n Tomato
    Sandwiches.................... 42
  Tomato Topper Canapés 21
Tortillas
  Cheesy Tortilla Turnovers 19
  Mexicali Eggs 53
Tuna and Macaroni Croquettes 37
Tuna Toastwiches 20

v

Veal
  Veal Parmigiana.................. 32
  Wiener Schnitzel 31
Vegetables 54-61
  Cottage Tomato Slices 60
  Crunchy-Coated Potato Patties 56
  Eggplant Italiano 61
  Golden Mushrooms 60
  Grilled Tomatoes 60
  Home-Style Potato Patties 57
  Quick Hash Browns 58
  Refried Beans.................... 58
  Sautéed Acorn Rings with
    Maple Glaze 59
  Sautéed Cabbage Wedges 61
  Sautéed Potato Slices 56
  Savory-Filled Squash Halves 59
  Smoky Potato Sticks 57
  Sno-Capped Sweets 58
  Speedy Potato Puffs 56

w

Wiener Schnitzel 31
Wieners 34
Wieners in Blankets 43
Wontons, Micro 23

y

Yams, see Sno-Capped Sweets 58

z

Zippy Barbecued Chops 30
Zucchini, see Chicken Breast Dinner .. 15